BODY
BRILLIANT

A TEENAGE GUIDE TO A :POSITIVE: BODY IMAGE

NICOLA MORGAN

First published in Great Britain in 2019 by The Watts Publishing Group
Text copyright © Nicola Morgan 2019
Cover and inside design copyright © Franklin Watts 2019

10 9 8 7 6 5 4 3 2 1

Managing editor: Victoria Brooker
Editor: Hayley Fairhead
Cover design: Thy Bui
Inside design: Rocket Design (East Anglia) Ltd
Inside illustrations: Shutterstock, p194 by Katherine Lynas

ISBN: 978 1 445 1 6736 7 (pbk)
ISBN: 978 1 445 1 6737 4 (e-book)

Printed and bound in Great Britain by Clays Ltd, Elcograf S.p.A.

Franklin Watts
An imprint of
Hachette Children's Group
Part of The Watts Publishing Group
Carmelite House
50 Victoria Embankment
London EC4Y 0DZ
An Hachette UK Company
www.hachette.co.uk
www.franklinwatts.co.uk

The website addresses (URLs) included in this book were
valid at the time of going to press. However, it is possible that
contents or addresses may have changed since the publication
of this book. No responsibility for any such changes can be
accepted by either the author or the Publisher.

Nicola Morgan is a leading expert in well-being and adolescence. For details of her work, events and contact, as well as many resources, go to: www.nicolamorgan.com

Acknowledgements

Body Brilliant is based on strong science and understanding of human behaviour but enriched by the lived experiences of real individuals. So many people of all ages answered my requests for insights that go beyond the science and I am grateful for their honesty and generosity in telling what were often poignant stories.

Special thanks to:

Dr Carrie Parris and the truly brilliant *Body Brilliant* team of students from Haggerston School, Hackney, London: Ahinoa, Alejandro, Arran, Ebele, Ellie-Marie, Joana, Jyotsna, Kate, Kawsar, Peter, Roheya, Sia, Shakir, Shannon, Thomas, Tony, Victor and Yasmin. Their words are in many places in the book (with names changed) and their interest, humour, honesty, support and genuine niceness brought fun to the process, as well as extra truth to the book. Chocolate, pizza and chips may also have featured...

My two wonderful research assistants, aka my nieces, Megan Morgan and Lucy Morgan. As recent graduates in Psychology and English, they had contacts in communities I otherwise couldn't have reached, as well as excellent research skills and strong ideas about positive body image.

I'm grateful for comments from Nicol Clayton, Specialist Paediatric Eating Disorders Dietician, Deborah Sandler from Cosmetic Support and Eva Musby, founder of Anorexia Family, as well as the expert insights from various other organisations and people with professional and personal experience of many topics covered in *Body Brilliant*.

Thanks to everyone at Hachette Children's Group who worked so hard on *Body Brilliant*, including having the idea in the first place!

Medical disclaimer

The information in this book is not intended to be a substitute for medical advice. If you have any worries about your mental or physical health, you should discuss it with a qualified medical doctor and follow their advice.

Content warning

This book covers topics which some readers might find distressing because of a personal experience. If any of the topics mentioned in the contents list makes you feel anxious, it would be a good idea to ask a trusted adult to support you.

Contents

Section Two

MAKING YOUR BODY BRILLIANT

5

INTRODUCTION

You already have a brilliant body. I know this, though I haven't met you. I don't mind whether you're tall or short, plump or skinny, darker or lighter-skinned, whether your nose is button-shaped or hooked, whether your eyes are round or narrow, how many limbs you own or what visible differences you have.

None of that makes your body brilliant. What makes it brilliant is what your body can do. And that's a lot. Think about what you can do that you couldn't do when you were born, all the skills you've had to learn and practise. Again, I don't know you, but I'm pretty sure you can do some (but not all) of these: run, skip, swim, play games, draw, write, read, operate a computer, bake, care for people, tie knots, somersault, have ideas, sing, act, dance, jump, throw a ball into a net, kick a football hard, touch a worm or a ladybird, tiptoe, stamp, smile, hug. Those are actions human bodies are capable of and you can do many of them. And you can do a lot of things not on that list, including things I can't.

> *"I worry how some of my friends think of their bodies. 'My shoulders are too broad' or 'My tummy is too fat'. We aren't 'too' anything! I know someone with anorexia so I know what it can do to you. I am guilty of comparing myself to others. I think we are comparing ourselves to other people more and more. Especially in an all-girls house. We compare our legs, boobs, noses and everything. We need to understand and accept that we all have different capabilities and appearance. Personality begins where comparison ends."*
>
> **Maddie, 16**

What we look like is utterly irrelevant compared to all that. Being taller or shorter or thinner or larger or more typically 'beautiful' than another person doesn't mean you can do those things better. Being slimmer or having whiter teeth does not make you a better or more successful person. Having a crooked smile or back or nose doesn't make you a crooked person. The weight of your body has nothing to do with the weight of your mind and the size of your belly nothing to do with the power of your brain. And if aspects of our physical bodies make some things easier or harder, so what? We can still do a lot with our bodies, whatever they look like.

Your body is the vehicle for your life. It gives you possibilities and choices, ambitions and power. It carries your dreams and allows you to try your best to make them come true.

If that was the end of the story, this would be the end of the book.

THE TROUBLE WITH HUMANS

The trouble with humans is that we can't ignore what we look like. Yes, we can learn to find appearance less important and to have a different opinion of it – one of the aims of this book – but we can't ignore it totally. Body image is something our brain creates. It's there, our mental picture of ourselves, whether we like it or not.

 "We all stand out in our own minds more than we actually do."
Rachel, 14

That can cause difficulties. Those difficulties can be small or dominate people's lives.

I want this book to help you see that what you look like is far, far less important than what you *are* like. It's not something I find easy myself but writing this book has helped me so I'm confident that reading it will help you!

Quick Check

WHAT DO I MEAN BY 'BODY IMAGE'?

Lots of people think that body image means what you look like.

No! 'Body image' is not what we look like but how we think and feel about what we look like – how we see ourselves and how we believe others see us.

Having a positive or negative body image describes how positively or negatively we view our appearance. It's also about how much mental energy we spend thinking about appearance compared to how much we think about doing and achieving more with the life we've been given. A positive body image means that we respect our body for what it can do. A negative body image means that we see ourselves negatively and we wish we could look different.

BODY BOOST

Throughout the book you'll find 'Body Boost' panels. Some of these are inspirational thoughts; some are ideas for activities to improve your body image or to deal with a negative situation; and some are practical tips for having a healthier lifestyle and looking after your brilliant body. Do as many of them as you can and you'll feel better about yourself.

The Body Boosts help you get the most out of *Body Brilliant*: boost your body, boost your life.

To start with, get a notebook (or open a new document on a computer). This will be your *Body Brilliant* book, where you can record tips, inspirational messages and ideas.

Once we understand how our body image happens, we can start to control it. We can learn to appreciate ourselves for who we are and what we can do. We can learn to respect our body and have a healthy lifestyle that keeps it as strong as possible – as brilliant as possible – so that we can do all the things we want to.

A positive body image is really important to well-being. If we spend too much head space feeling negative about what we look like, we can miss opportunities to live the best, most exciting and most successful life possible. And feeling bad about our appearance sometimes makes us less likely to look after our body. If we don't respect ourselves, we may make less healthy choices. We may veer from self-neglect to self-obsession.

People of any age can (and often do) have negative body image. As I started to talk to people of all ages, including my age, I was struck by how negative so many of us feel and what unhealthy messages we share about weight in particular. The adults around you might fuel your worries about weight and shape by unintentionally sharing their own negativity. I hope this book will help adults see how their own well-meaning concerns can be unhelpful and even damaging. And how focusing on health, not appearance, is always the way to go, whatever age or size you are.

BODY BOOST

Start thinking about positive slogans about body image. Things like, 'My body is my super-power' or 'Beauty is not skin-deep' or 'My body, my life, my business'. Gradually work out which is your favourite.

It can become your motto, which you'll say to yourself any time your body image is challenged by negative thoughts or other people's comments.

"I certainly found myself comparing my body to others and judging myself against them. I would see people and constantly wonder why they were all beautiful and I wasn't. It seemed to me that all the other girls had perfect body shapes and luscious hair, and I didn't. It made me feel as if I wasn't good enough, all because of how I looked."
Iona

WHY IS THIS BOOK ESPECIALLY FOR TEENAGERS IF BODY IMAGE AFFECTS EVERYONE?

Adolescence is a stage of life that brings enormous changes. The changes can be exciting and positive: more freedom, independence, skills and knowledge. Or they can be upsetting and confusing. I call adolescence a perfect storm of change because everything is changing fast: your brain, mind, friends, environment, fears, ambitions, desires, pressures. And your body, appearance and how you feel about yourself. Many teenagers say that when they were younger they never thought about their appearance, but that it all changed as they reached secondary school.

It can be disconcerting seeing your physical changes and confusing as your brain tries to keep up with what you look like.

"My body image is sometimes positive and sometimes negative. In school, I don't think about my appearance because I focus on work. At home, I would like to look fitter. Some of my friends spend a lot of time on exercise and doing their make-up. Some are obsessed with looking fitter or skinnier – boys and girls."
Bella, 15

Not all teenagers have big problems with body image but many do. This book is for you. But, if you're lucky enough not to have worries about your body or appearance, there are two other reasons you might find *Body Brilliant* useful. First, it will help you understand the problems some of your friends (and parents!) may have. Second, it has masses of sensible advice, to help everyone have the most brilliantly healthy body possible. Health is far more important than beauty because health allows your body to do what you want to do.

 "Some of my friends spend a lot of time and money on how they look. I don't. Lots of people, boys and girls, are quite obsessed with how they look."
Stella, 15

DIFFERENT CHALLENGES

Some people have more risk of negative body image than others and some people suffer more because of it. People with disabilities or visible differences might struggle more with how they feel about their appearance. Eating disorders and self-harming are often associated with a negative body image.

Questioning gender can sometimes challenge one's body image in a specific set of ways. Being 'different' in any way – taller or shorter than the people around you; having an accident that dramatically changes your body; struggling with fluctuating weight; being teased or bullied because of some perceived 'flaw' in your looks; really hating yourself or something about you – all these and more can make it really, really hard not to focus on appearance.

In addition, growing up amongst people of a different skin colour or ethnic background from our own might sometimes create conflict between two sets of 'ideals'. Anything that makes you look different from the people you spend time with can make you self-conscious of your appearance.

I'll be tackling all those challenges, and more, in this book.

BODY BOOST

In your notebook, write down the heading:
'My body is brilliant because...' –
now fill that space with all the amazing
things your body can DO.

→ IS THIS A MODERN PROBLEM?

It certainly feels that negative body image is a bigger problem nowadays. It's likely that the internet and social media partly explain that, though I'll also show you how they can be a force for good. We are bombarded with images that we're supposed to aspire to, many of which can only be achieved if we have cosmetic surgery or pay a lot of money. It's incredibly easy to feel inadequate and dissatisfied.

> *"My 20-year-old daughter has just started watching Vampire Diaries and has actually looked up the actresses' BMI as she says watching the programmes make her depressed because the women in it all look so perfect. She is an incredibly bright individual but with very negative body image issues, though she's a perfectly normal shape with curves. My 14-year-old daughter is very feminist in outlook and hates stereotyping so is less concerned about appearance, but she has always had more confidence than my older one. Lower confidence means concern about image comes before attitude/ability/achievement."*
> **Julia**

This book aims to help you not feel like that! This book aims to show you that your body is brilliant even with all its so-called flaws. They are not flaws, but part of what make you individual and human, not a plastic doll or robot.

About the Word 'Fat'

The word 'fat' is often used as an insult. This is wrong! Fat is a natural and important part of our bodies, evolved to protect us and provide fuel. Healthy people come in many shapes and sizes, including curvaceous. And beauty comes in many shapes and sizes, too.

Yes, you can have too much fat and you can have too little of it – both extremes can make you less fit and more likely to suffer various illnesses. But someone who is bigger than another person is not necessarily less healthy (or attractive). Being large can make you strong; and a slim person can be unhealthy. It's all about keeping within sensible boundaries. Only a relevant expert can say whether someone is within those boundaries, as it's not just about what the scales say, but more complex and individual than that. And if they say that you have more fat than is healthy, you need expert support to find a healthier life-style.

 "Fat-shaming affects mental health and makes people feel terrible. We should let our friends know how we feel because insults and teasing don't help someone be healthier."
Nana Kwame, 14

Fat-shaming – making people feel guilty or lazy or stupid because their body is larger than someone else's – is cruel, ignorant and unhelpful. Research shows that making people ashamed of their weight is more likely to make them put on weight than lose it. When someone feels ashamed of their body, they may not value it enough to treat it well.

"All my adult life I've had a hang-up about my bottom. I am average height and average build and not particularly overweight, though I'd be happy to lose a bit. When I was about 12 or 13 I was walking home from school when some boys shouted, 'Oi, fat arse'. I was no larger than most of my peers. But the embarrassment stuck and from then part of my brain would not let go of that label. I would tell myself it wasn't true and that they were just being mean, but another voice would repeat their words.

"Later, boyfriends and then my husband told me they loved my bottom, but instead I believe the taunts of some teenage boys nearly 40 years ago. Even now, if I wear tight fitting jeans or leggings, I team them with a long top. It's the feature that I'm most self-conscious about."
Sarah

So 'fat' is not an insult or a judgement. It's part of us. Having some fat covering certain areas of our bodies – and some areas more than others – is natural and healthy, nothing to be afraid of or to wish away. And certainly nothing to be ashamed of.

How
Body Brilliant
Works

The first section of *Body Brilliant* is called 'All In the Mind' because body image is all in the mind. I'll share how your brain creates your body image. I'll give you tools so that you can start to have a better body image.

But *Body Brilliant* is about your actual body as well as how your mind sees it. The second section – 'Your Brilliant Body' – has practical ways to make your body the best it can be.

This book is a guidebook for living healthily and actively, eating and enjoying wonderful food, using your body better and making it stronger and healthier, and giving your body and mind everything they need to live a long, happy and fulfilled life. It's a guidebook for worrying less about what you look like and caring more about what your body can do. It's OK to want to look good, but only if that desire comes from truly respecting your body, not because you're trying to compete or copy artificial ideals and set yourself unreasonable targets.

We have a responsibility to our bodies, a responsibility to make good choices and to make those choices because we respect ourselves, not because someone said we should. Our choices, whether big ones like deciding to take up swimming as a sport, or small ones like deciding to go swimming today, make a difference. They make a difference to our mind and to our body, because those two things are incredibly tightly connected.

Body Brilliant shows you why you should make good choices and how, and empowers you to make your body truly, positively brilliant!

Content warning:

Some people find it very distressing to read about certain topics of which they have intense personal experience. This book includes subjects such as gender questioning, eating disorders and body dysmorphia, which some readers might find upsetting. I have done my best to write as sensitively as possible, after a great deal of research and talking to people with lived experience, but I also believe that talking about distressing things with someone you trust is generally a good way to become more resilient. So, if anything worries you, please discuss it with someone who knows you and your situation and get whatever support you need.

Section One
ALL IN THE MIND

This section looks at how your mind creates a body image, why having a positive body image is important and all the many things that can make a negative body image. We will look at challenging situations and by the end you'll have a really good understanding of the factors that *can* make positive body image difficult. It will also include mental and practical strategies to help you have the most positive body image possible.

 "At 10 years old, my daughter is not concerned about body image and I'd love to keep it that way. Every morning, I tell her she is beautiful. I also tell her that she is kind, hard-working and creative, because it's all true."
Shaheen

LET'S UNDERSTAND BODY IMAGE

WHAT *EXACTLY* IS BODY IMAGE?

Our body image is how we mentally answer the question, 'What do people see when they see me?' I say 'mentally' because this is not something you normally say out loud and it would be difficult to put into words. It's more like a picture.

Our answer will depend on lots of things, including what people around us look like. So, if we are with people who are much older or younger than us, or taller or shorter, or thinner or fatter, or who have a different skin colour or some other aspect of appearance that makes us noticeable or different, that way in which we stand out will inform a large part of how we mentally see ourselves.

 "In my early teens, my very beautiful godmother and an au pair I admired each commented that I needed to watch out for my bottom. The implication was that I would need to control my weight to stop it being too big. I used to

watch my reflection in windows and hate my silhouette. Photos at a wedding altered my entire memory of the event. I had liked my outfit, felt pretty. But the photos showed a disproportionate bottom. I'm now 49 and I still hate my shape. I would like to ask those people what was the point of their comments? I'd like to tell myself that I was gorgeous and that it is a crying shame that I was so self-critical. I still am but I now have so much appetite for life, for the things I want to do, and to be there for those I love. What I look like is of so little relevance. I feel deeply lucky to still be alive and doing what I want to do. That is what the body is for, not to gain acceptance of others."

Frances

So, standing out is a big factor in how we answer, 'What do people see when they see me?'

Believing that we stand out amongst people we see a lot can make us feel negative about how we look. On the other hand, some people love to stand out and some differences are easier to feel positive about. This means that standing out can have a positive or negative effect on body image.

WHAT *EXACTLY* DO WE MEAN BY 'POSITIVE' OR 'NEGATIVE' BODY IMAGE? ←

Someone with a positive body image:

+ Is reasonably happy about the way they look. They may not think they look fantastic but they respect themselves and believe that appearance is not as important as abilities and character.

➕ Has a reasonably accurate impression of their size and appearance – not thinking they're overweight when they're thin, for example, or that their nose is unusually big when it's quite average.

➕ Doesn't spend time wishing they looked different.

Someone with a positive body image focuses on what they can do rather than how they look.

> 💬 "If people make a comment about my appearance, I couldn't care less as I don't believe in being offended. I think I have a positive body image but I'm not here to get friends based on how I look."
> **Charlie, 13**

Someone with a negative body image:

➖ Dislikes their body or one or more aspects of it

➖ Believes that they look 'worse' in some way than they do

➖ Spends a lot of headspace thinking negatively about how they look.

People with a negative body image may do unhealthy things to try to change their body, such as restricting food, over-exercising, or spending too much money and time on cosmetic products or procedures. On the other hand, they may not try to look after themselves, believing they're not worth it.

> 💬 "It is hard to imagine a world when being mixed-race was unusual. In 1960s London, I barely saw any people like me even in my north London primary school. In Wales my brother and I were clearly and completely different. Very often other kids would want to touch my skin. I have always felt – like many mixed-race people – neither one thing nor another."
> **Catherine**

WHERE DOES BODY IMAGE COME FROM AND IS IT RELIABLE?

Our body image is only what we *think* people see when they see us. Often, we're wrong. Your mental picture has been built gradually since you were born and will continue to change. It's affected by things people say, the people and images that surround you, and your own observations, filtered through your opinions and emotions.

You've looked at your changing body and face countless times in mirrors and photos. You've compared your appearance to the bodies and faces around you. You're making constant changes to the mental image, depending on all these cues around you, every day, over and over again. You might not think about this consciously, but you can't help doing it. You're human!

It is your mind doing all that and your mind doesn't measure accurately, as you're about to find out.

> "I have been very tall all my life and have had to get used to the insults, even though I still sometimes find it annoying. I'd rather disappear into the crowd than stand out. I think the world was built for average people, which I'm not, and that is a challenge for me."
> **Harris, 14**

Let's understand body image   **27**

Here's how we build our body image:

Looking in the mirror

This is the obvious way most of us get information to build a mental picture of ourselves. Most of us have looked in a mirror several times a day, since we were very young.

BODY BOOST

Do you look in a mirror too much? Count how many times you look during one day. Next day, see if you can cut that by half. Now, think of one thing about your appearance that you like. Next time you are about to look in a mirror, remind yourself to look at that. The more you focus on what you're happy about, the less you'll think about what you don't like. You can change how you think, one thought at a time.

Sensing ourselves directly

We can see parts of our body in other ways than through a mirror and we can feel our waist or thighs, touch our nose, ears, hair. People who don't have the sense of sight still have a body image, a mental picture of what they look like. I'll talk a bit more about blind people and body image on pages 151–7.

Photos

Cameras do lie! Shadows, light, angles all make a difference. Any irregularities will be highlighted. I have a very irregular face, which I notice much more in photos than in a mirror.

Videos

These are not reliable either. Many people are quite self-conscious being filmed, so may not be looking natural; and, as with photos, a lot depends on lighting and shadows.

But all the above methods of self-measurement are straightforward compared to the fascinating ones that follow.

'Confirmation bias'

We see what confirms our opinions. We see ourselves through a distorting filter: our mind. For example, if we believe, 'I'm overweight' or 'My jaw is horrible', often that's the main thing we see in the photo or mirror. If another photo or angle shows a flattering image, we dismiss that as a fluke and the next image that shows our supposed flaw will confirm what we already believed.

What other people say – especially negative things

If someone once made a negative comment about your appearance, that can really damage your mental image. Most of us can probably remember someone once saying something negative. For me, it was two things: my knobbly knees, not helped by the fact that at my school in assembly we had to stand in front of the rest of the school wearing our skirts just above the knee, which is very exposing for someone who thinks she has knobbly knees! And my lack of breasts – I was skinny and younger than everyone else and I felt I looked different. I now know that body parts naturally come in a wide range of sizes and those sizes mean nothing, but people's comments can be horribly powerful.

"I try not to listen to comments but sometimes things get through my 'wall'. Sometimes I get upset when I look at myself."
Kaid, 15

Negative comments don't all become major problems, but plenty of people with eating disorders or severe anxiety about their bodies can trace the cause to 'something someone said'. When these comments come at vulnerable times, such as during adolescence or anxiety about school or parental break-up, they can trigger lasting problems. You'll find more about this in the chapters on 'Eating Disorders and Self-Harm' and 'Body Dysmorphic Disorder'.

 "In Year 7, I was called ugly, fat and that my hair was like witches' hair."
Maria, 15

How truthful you think someone is being

If your parents or carers tell you you're perfect, you might think, 'Well, they would – they're my parents.' Many people distrust compliments from friends, but believe the comments of strangers or people they don't much like. It's the wrong way around!

 "My daughter, now 15, was a very pretty, picture-perfect child, with long, thick, glossy, blonde hair, huge blue eyes, long lashes etc. People often commented positively on her looks, even strangers. At around 4 years old, she came home from nursery one day having cut her eyelashes off. Even now that makes me feel wobbly to think of it. She made angry and distressed requests that people would stop touching her hair, stop calling her a princess (which

I never had). Now a teenager, she has short hair and rejects the dolly aesthetic of her generation. No make-up, tight clothes or short skirts."

Frances

Mood

We see ourselves more negatively when we're feeling low. When life's going well or you've just had some success, it's easy to forget about aspects of your appearance you don't like.

People who are suffering from depression tend to dwell on negatives; if appearance is one of their negatives, they're likely to notice that more when they are feeling worst. If you know someone who is feeling low, remind them that mood is colouring their thoughts.

BODY BOOST

Mood affects body image so, if you're feeling down, do something healthy to raise your mood. Choose something that will make you feel good afterwards, too, not just for a short burst while you're doing it. For example, go for a walk, meet a friend, sit in the sunshine for a few minutes, watch a funny or feel-good film. You'll be glad you did them afterwards and they feel good at the time.

Hormones

Some girls and women report feeling more negative about their bodies before and sometimes during their periods[1]. It's possible that female hormones make a difference to how you see yourself. We don't know if there's a similar effect from male hormones.

We just aren't good at being objective about our bodies!

We really aren't! This is so interesting that I am going to say more.

→ HOW OUR BRAIN GETS IT WRONG

There's a skill our brains have called proprioception. It's sometimes called the 'position sense', because it's a sense of where the various parts of our body are even when we're not looking at them. Close your eyes for a moment. Hold your hands out. You know exactly what position they're in and you have a sense of how big they are. That's proprioception. We use it all the time: when we're walking or running we don't look at our feet to make sure they're doing the right thing: we know they are. Proprioception can go wrong: people who've had a limb amputated can often feel it as though it's still there – 'missing limb syndrome' or 'phantom limb syndrome'.

Missing limb syndrome shows that body image doesn't just come from what we can see. A person with the amputated leg can see that it's not there. There are more complex things going on, though experts aren't sure of the exact cause.

....

1   Article in *Bustle* by Rachel Krantz https://www.bustle.com/articles/134402-the-one-pms-symptom-nobody-talks-about

Two very rare conditions show how inaccurately a very few people experience their bodies:

★ Asomatognosia is when patients don't see or recognise one side or part of their body.

★ Somatoparaphrenia is when a patient completely denies that a part of their body belongs to them.

The brain is fascinating!

Then there's Alice in Wonderland syndrome, which can happen in two ways: the patient may suddenly feel enormous or tiny, or may experience objects as seeming far away. I had this as a child when I had a fever. I remember it vividly. This can also be part of a migraine attack and it may be what Lewis Carroll experienced, inspiring the story of *Alice in Wonderland*.

Those conditions are medical, but healthy people don't have accurate ways of measuring their body size, either.

> "I don't really worry about my body shape. My friend and I joke about our shape being like bagels! We did try dieting once – it didn't last long."
>
> **Daisy, 14**

Research shows most people view themselves as larger than they are. A study[2] by University College London got people to place one hand under a board so they couldn't see it and point on the board to where they thought various parts of their hand were. On average, people guessed their hand was two thirds wider and a third longer than it really was.

2   Research by Dr Matthew Longo, described in PsychCentral: https://psychcentral.com/news/2010/06/17/our-brains-distort-our-own-body-image/14665.html

There may be cultural differences. Various studies suggest differences between how accurately and positively different ethnic groups typically judge their weight, with African-American women seeming more often to have a more accurate *and* positive body image than white American women. But other studies show women from a range of backgrounds aiming for a thin ideal and seeing themselves as fatter than they are. (Remember that such studies can only show what is typical for the people being studied: many people will be different.)

Later, I'll talk about Body Dysmorphic Disorder (see chapter seven), where sufferers believe that they or some part of them are 'disgusting', despite their appearance being completely typical.

"Ever since the birth of my second child two years ago, I have excess tummy skin/flab and I hate it. The rest of me is so toned. No amount of exercise and dieting seems to shift it.

"About a year ago, I got the dreaded question 'Are you pregnant again?' I was horrified and went home and cried. It wasn't just in my head: I really did look pregnant. I'm 38 and never cared how much I weigh so this is new territory. I feel cheated because I see myself as fit – I ran a 3 hour 49 minute marathon very recently! But now I have ridiculous worries, like people seeing my tummy and thinking 'How can she run with that fat on her?' Why do I worry about what other people think? Is it this horrid stereotype that for a woman to be attractive she needs to be slim? The silly thing is that I wouldn't even notice my tummy if I had more weight on the rest of me!"

Eleanor

BODY BOOST

Praise yourself. Respect your strength, your skilful fingers, your speed, how well you can sometimes kick or throw a ball. And your invisible skills: your honesty, kindness, determination, resilience, ideas.

Write a couple of those strengths on a piece of paper and stick it above your mirror: 'I am a great friend', 'I am a brilliant listener', 'I have an amazing imagination', 'I am good at maths', 'I can run fast'.

I have
an amazing
imagination

Unconscious comparison with people nearby – 'Serial dependence'

Serial dependence[3] is fascinating. If you've just been looking at bodies of a certain size – perhaps thinner than average – you are likely to judge your body (or another body you look at) as fatter than if you had been looking at larger bodies.

A brilliant illustration came in a study[4] in which 103 female psychology students had to say how fat or thin a picture of a body seemed to them. The answers depended heavily on the previous image. If they'd just seen a larger one, they were likely to give the next image a 'slimmer' rating than if they'd just seen a smaller one.

Serial dependence is likely to affect us all. If we spend time with people who are slimmer than us or we keep seeing skinny images online, we're likely to compare ourselves with those images and see ourselves as larger than we actually are.

Everything is relative. One person's body is not 'big' or 'small' but only 'bigger or smaller than those ones', and 'those ones' are likely to be the ones you're familiar with.

....

3   https://particle.scitech.org.au/people/looking-good-your-brain-might-be-playing-tricks-on-you/

4   Research by Dr Matthew Longo, described in PsychCentral: https://psychcentral.com/news/2010/06/17/our-brains-distort-our-own-body-image/14665.html

Comparison with media images and advertising

That last point links with what many people believe has the most damaging effect on body image: media obsession with unrealistic, digitally-altered images of 'perfection'.

This is a big topic, so I'll cover it in the next chapter: Different Times, Different Cultures.

Can parents and other adults be part of the problem?

Absolutely! When I asked people to provide thoughts and experiences for this book, I was struck by the number of adults who were strongly negatively affected by comments from their parents. Parents can be very anxious about their children's weight and can very easily (and quite accidentally) promote messages that lead their child to have a negative body image. Parents have a responsibility to help their children be within a healthy weight range, but it's easy to say the wrong thing and trigger an unhealthy attitude to food.

"I have always viewed myself as big. I was taller than all my friends and my big sister. People commented on that a lot. I was a sensitive child who only really wanted to melt into the background. When I was around 12 one uncle joked about my height during a family get together. In a shoe shop, a smirking shop assistant asked if I'd tried the ski department. I had to bite back tears. I was given

male roles in school plays and put at the back of class photographs. There was never anything positive about my size. I felt ashamed.

"The thing is, looking at the few photographs of myself from then, I wasn't a ginormous freak: I was lovely. I was 5ft 11 at 15 and with confidence and support I could have been a catwalk model. Instead, I tried to look shorter by stooping, my anxiety grew and I began to comfort eat. My weight has gone up and down ever since."
Hazel

But parents also suffer from their own poor body image and may pass that message onto their children even if they say nothing at all about their child's weight. 'I need to lose some weight before our holiday,' 'Oh, look at this horrible roll of fat,' 'I look terrible today,' 'No, I can't have that cake – a moment on the lips, a life-time on the hips!'

"My whole life my body image has been influenced by my mother. My life has been dominated by Mum telling me I'd get arms like hers, and legs like hers. When I was probably pre-teenage, we'd be out shopping and my mum would spot a very fat woman and would say to me, 'Am I as fat as that?' She passed her insecurities on to me."
Darrell

If parents want their children to have a healthy attitude to food – which means enjoying food, eating a wide range of things, having celebratory meals with friends and family and fuelling body and brain with all that the world has to offer – they have to model that behaviour themselves.

If you notice your parents making negative comments about their own bodies, **call them out** on it and start a discussion!

BODY BOOST

When you hear anyone commenting about appearance (whether their own or someone else's), drag the conversation back to personality and achievement, not shape and appearance. Call out your parents or other adults when they say things like, 'Oh, I'm so fat today'. Ban fat-talk at home, amongst your friends and in your head! And not just negative comments: all comments about appearance. Make people notice how often they talk about appearance. Start a revolution where we focus on character!

Even school 'healthy eating' programmes can be a problem. Of course, education about how to make great choices is really important, but sometimes schools do this by removing the items viewed as unhealthy.

Removing choices doesn't help you make good choices: it makes it more likely that you come to see some foods as forbidden and therefore perhaps more attractive. You may be more likely to 'reward' yourself with the forbidden food later. It induces guilt around food, which is not what we want.

Healthy eating is about loving great food and being able to choose a wide range to suit the occasion and to suit your body's needs.

WHY IS POSITIVE BODY IMAGE SO IMPORTANT?

Think about weight as an example, because that's the issue that most people think of when they think of body image. There's plenty of research that a negative body image leads to more problems with excess weight gain than a positive body image does.

Not just for girls

 Some research shows that teenage girls often opt out of activities such as swimming and even speaking up in class, because of unhappiness with their weight. This can happen for boys, too, but more studies have been done on girls than boys, because body image problems have traditionally been seen as more common in females. But boys have problems, too, and where research exists it tends to confirm this. Body image is not a female issue! We all have a body image and for very many of us it causes unhappiness and low self-esteem that affect our daily lives.

> "Society increasingly seeks validation from external sources. I can see the problems this causes the women in my life. For an exam assignment, I am designing a range of lingerie that addresses current body image issues. I have chosen lingerie because it is something women choose although other people usually won't see it. Through my research I have discovered that if women feel comfortable in their choice of underwear it can be empowering. I want to explore the idea that confidence and beauty need to come from within, not without."
>
> **Savannah, 17**

Body image affects how we feel about ourselves, our self-esteem. It affects how we eat, exercise, relate to friends, go for opportunities and every aspect of our well-being. Well-being affects how we aspire and succeed. All because of a body image that could be very different from what our body actually looks like.

Don't waste your mental space

If our body image is only slightly different from reality, that's not too much of a problem. But if it is very different you can have big problems. If you think you're too large when you're not, you're likely either to eat too little (and lose too much weight) or exercise too much (and again lose too much weight or damage your joints) or spend too much mental energy and time thinking and worrying about your weight instead of getting on with other aspects of life. If your body image severely exaggerates your perceived 'flaws' – whether you think you've got too much or too little flesh in whichever places, or anything else you don't like about your appearance – again too much of your mental space could be occupied by this.

If you measure your worth as a human being according to how you look, you aren't doing yourself justice and you can become overwhelmed by a quite unjustified self-hatred or unfair self-criticism. You can think you don't deserve to be loved or to be successful. That is so very wrong.

And you can waste hours, months, years, and enormous energy and ability, focusing on your body instead of your potential as a fantastic, talented, determined, valuable human being.

That's what I hope this book can stop. You'll find chapters devoted to those big problems that some people can have. I hope you don't have them but, if you do, I hope this book can start to help. Or if you have a friend with these problems, it can help you understand them.

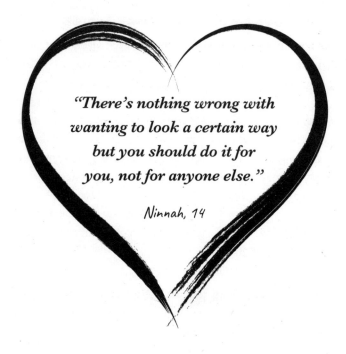

"There's nothing wrong with wanting to look a certain way but you should do it for you, not for anyone else."

Ninnah, 14

Summing up

Body image is how we think the world sees us. The picture is formed in our minds, built up from masses of data: seeing ourselves in mirrors and photos and in the flesh, things people say, comparing ourselves with the people around us and the images we see on television and online. Our body image is usually not accurate and sometimes it's very inaccurate.

We should try to view our appearance as the least important thing about us but that's very hard to do sometimes. Understanding as much as possible what's going on in our minds and in the world around us will help us come to a place where we can think: I have a brilliant body because of all the things it can do; how it looks is much less important than what it can do.

RESOURCES FOR
THIS CHAPTER

ONLINE

Get the Facts:
www.getthefacts.health.wa.gov.au/our-bodies/body-image

Informative Powerpoint for adults and teenagers:
www.macmh.org/wp-content/uploads/2014/05/18_Gallivan_Teens-social-media-body-image-presentation-H-Gallivan-Spring-2014.pdf

Good introduction in Psychology Today: www.psychologytoday.com/us/blog/eyes-the-brain/201002/body-image

Serial dependence: https://particle.scitech.org.au/people/looking-good-your-brain-might-be-playing-tricks-on-you/

'Size is largely in the mind: how your body image can change in two minutes' http://theconversation.com/size-is-largely-in-the-mind-how-your-body-image-can-change-in-two-minutes-62428

Positive body image:

Dove Self-Esteem Project: www.dove.com/uk/dove-self-esteem-project/school-workshops-on-body-image-confident-me.html

Be Real Campaign: www.berealcampaign.co.uk/

Free Being Me: https://free-being-me.com/

Bare Reality, by Laura Dodsworth, showing real men and women: www.barereality.net/

Ashley Graham: 'Plus Size? More Like My Size':
www.youtube.com/watch?v=xAgawjzimjc

Iskra Lawrence: 'Ending the Pursuit of Perfection':
www.youtube.com/watch?v=GR_hq7OVzHU

Megan Jayne Crabbe writes as BodyPosiPanda:
www.bodyposipanda.com/

Especially for girls:

A Mighty Girl has lots of books and other things for all ages: www.amightygirl.com

Adios Barbie is a brilliant and wide-ranging site: www.adiosbarbie.com

Hardy Girls Healthy Women: http://hghw.org/

Especially for boys:

Very Well Family: www.verywellfamily.com/male-body-image-your-son-and-his-body-3200812

A Guy's Guide to Body Image on TeenHealth: https://kidshealth.org/en/teens/male-bodyimage.html

BOOKS

(Remember: reading about certain topics can trigger distress in affected people.)

Fiction

Wintergirls by Laurie Halse Anderson. The author says *Wintergirls* '... forced me to deal with my own body image problems.' Q&A: http://madwomanintheforest.com/wintergirls-qa/

Big Bones by Laura Dockrill – BB loves her body however big it is, but she knows she needs to exercise to be healthier, not to lose weight.

Non-fiction

Body Positive Power by Megan Jayne Crabbe – activist in the body positive movement

Body Image Survival Guide (for parents) – by Marci Warhaft-Nadler

chapter *two*

DIFFERENT TIMES, DIFFERENT CULTURES

'Beauty is in the eye of the beholder' is a saying you'll probably have heard. It is from well over two thousand years ago! The philosopher, Plato, said it in 360BCE but it's as true today as it ever was: that there is no one fixed true thing that is called beauty. Beauty is how each individual mind judges what it sees. And each of us is a product of the time and culture we're in, so how we judge beauty changes according to that.

BODY BOOST

Make a poster to illustrate 'Beauty is in the eye of the beholder' – the fact that we all like different things and that what we like is partly to do with where and when we live.

We often forget that our tastes and opinions are just tastes and opinions, changing over time and between cultures. It's helpful to be reminded that they are not 'the truth'.

The media, advertising, art and fashion industries offer us ideals and brainwash us into aspiring to them. Some aspirations can be healthy, such as wanting to be stronger so that we can run or swim faster. But they can be less healthy, such as wanting our skin to be darker or lighter; or wanting to be slimmer just to fit into a smaller pair of jeans or conform to a shape that someone else has told us to copy; or wanting our hair to be straighter, because of fashion.

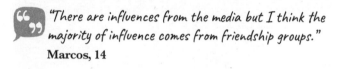 *"There are influences from the media but I think the majority of influence comes from friendship groups."*
Marcos, 14

But there is no One True Ideal body shape or colour or appearance. There are only trends. Any time we look at a model or photo or watch an actor and envy their appearance, we are victims of an incredibly subjective set of ideals, not some overall definition of gorgeousness. These 'ideals' are relative to the time or culture that we're in now. They mean nothing more.

Each culture and generation has its own 'ideals': the 'desired look' which people in that culture or generation feel drawn to aspire to.

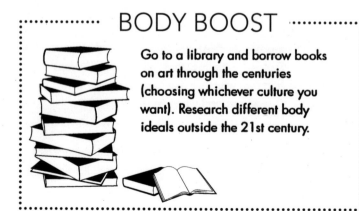

BODY BOOST

Go to a library and borrow books on art through the centuries (choosing whichever culture you want). Research different body ideals outside the 21st century.

Here are a few examples of how ideals have changed over the centuries.

CHANGING BEAUTY IDEALS FOR WOMEN

In the US and Europe, until about the 20th century, fashions came and went but mostly the ideal for women was to be curvy and well-covered in fat. Look at paintings by Rubens, the 17th century Dutch painter. In fact, 'rubenesque' now describes women who are full-figured.

In the late 19th century in the US, artist Charles Dana Gibson drew women known as the 'Gibson girls' with thin waists and large breasts. Almost no women naturally have this shape, so women had to wear tight corsets to shrink their waists.

Similarly, in the UK, Victorian women would be laced into their corsets, with someone pulling the laces tight behind them. It was quite common for women to faint. The 'delicate' Victorian lady who kept fainting was probably a victim of her underwear! This fashion could damage internal organs and made it impossible to be active and fit.

In the 1920s, women often wore bras to flatten their breasts; clothing was designed to make them look thin and boyish.

This 'boyish' look faded in Hollywood from the 1930s to 50s, with Marilyn Monroe as an obvious example of the curvy new ideal. Adverts encouraged women to put weight on. There's one poster showing a woman saying, 'Men wouldn't look at me when I was skinny – but since I gained 10 pounds this new easy way I have all the dates I want.'

Then, back came thin – very thin. From the 1960s and 70s, in countries which followed Western fashions, the trend was über-thin, with models looking pale, weak and ill. In the 70s and 80s, tanned skin and 'big hair' came in and there was a health and fitness craze, with a lean, bronzed, strong look. But in the '90s and into the 2000s, thin was back, with the 'size zero' look that encouraged dangerous starvation.

In the early 21st century, Western aspirations for women included a flat stomach (which is unlikely, as we do have internal organs!), large breasts and buttocks and the 'thigh gap', the gap that some women have between their thighs when they stand with their feet together. The thigh gap is not to do with weight, but is a function of bone structure. They are neither good nor bad but trying to get one if you don't have one is pointless and risks unhealthy eating and over-exercising.

There was a major backlash against the thigh gap. When it was discovered that a major US store had digitally added a thigh gap onto a young model in a bathing suit, the company had to apologise. The industry, it seemed had gone too far.

CHANGING BEAUTY IDEALS FOR MEN? ←

Men have also had changing ideals to follow. Whether it's facial hair trimmed in a certain shape, developing a 'ripped' six-pack, slimming or bulking, being tall or short, looking masculine or feminine – the desirability of these has changed over generations and cultures.

There have been times in history when being fat showed wealth. It was a sign that you could afford to eat a lot and had servants to do physical work. Henry VIII of England is an obvious example.

Physical strength and fitness have also always been aspirations for men, though, as they are today. In previous times, it would mean you could ride your horse better than anyone, throw a spear or wield a sword more effectively, beat your opponents in fights. Nowadays, looking fit and strong is partly about physical health and strength, but for some it's more about looks than health or function.

> *"I have a more positive than negative body image because I like feeling strong and I can see my muscles building up. I would like to put on muscle as I think that is what people prefer these days. A skinny guy isn't seen as being as 'good' as a muscled one."*
> **Harris, 14**

For young men today, the big aspiration is visible muscle. If this meant just doing a bit more exercise, that wouldn't be a problem, because exercise is great for health and strength. But when it involves special supplements, protein drinks or over-exercising, and when it's about appearance more than health, it can lead to obsessive behaviours and disordered eating. I'll talk more about this when I discuss gym culture (pages 84–7 and again in chapter nine).

"People sometimes comment that I'm too skinny. I try not to be affected but sometimes it makes me feel unconfident. I have friends who exercise a lot but I don't think this is for appearance, more for health."
Daniel, 14

Facial hair has gone in and out of fashion over the centuries. When I was younger, beards were seen as scruffy and 'unprofessional'. The unshaven look was just for holidays. Now, beards are very fashionable. But growing a beard is a lot more complicated than it used to be, too! Different styles – hipster, goatee, royale, circle or others – label you. Facial grooming products are a huge market and keeping a chosen style is not cheap.

BODY POSITIVITY

Around 2015, the body positivity movement arose, to encourage people to celebrate whatever size they were. When British model, Charli Howard, after years of being shamed by her agency into losing even more weight while she struggled with eating disorders, wrote an angry open letter on Facebook in 2015, her post went viral. Her agency had been trying to force her to 'slim' to an impossible hip-size and she'd had enough of the abuse suffered by models. At the time weighing seven stone, she said, "I cannot miraculously shave my hip-bones down, just to fit into a sample size piece of clothing or to meet 'agency standards'. I have fought nature for a long time, because you've deemed my body shape 'too curvaceous,' but I've recently begun to love my shape." One result was the rise of the body positivity movement.

Love your body and be healthy

But there was a backlash to that, too. There are two main arguments. First, some people feel that body positivity celebrates large bodies more than smaller bodies. The slogan 'real women have curves' undermines those women who are naturally uncurvy. Real women (and men) come in a wide variety of shapes and sizes, and curvy is no more 'real' than skinny.

The other argument is that most medical people agree that being very overweight is unhealthy (as is being very underweight), risking serious illnesses that can limit lives and quality of life. Some people feel that the body positivity movement risks encouraging people to be larger than is healthy. So, the line between loving our bodies as they are and trying to be healthy is tricky. (I hope that by the end of this book you'll have picked up the messages that will keep you caring for your body, keeping it healthy, strong and respected. Remember that there is a very wide range of perfectly healthy, wonderful body shapes.)

Nowadays, there's also the world of cosmetic procedures that involve altering the body with implants for breasts and buttocks, lip-fillers and muscle relaxants, such as the botulinum toxin (botox), as well as all manner of other expensive treatments to change our appearance cosmetically. Kim Kardashian and her younger sister Kylie Jenner (who, in 2019, at the age of 21, had made a billion US dollars from her vast make-up empire and millions of followers) are examples of the fashion for an artificially tiny waist, large breasts and bum, along with a flat stomach.

I wonder what the next fashion will be? Will you follow it or rise above it and focus on having a brilliant life?

Differences around the World

Meanwhile, different countries and cultures have different ideals. This was brilliantly illustrated when the project 'Perceptions of Perfection across Borders' asked graphic designers from 18 countries to digitally alter one photo of a woman[5] by *'making her, in their opinion, more attractive to other citizens in their country.'* The designers then did the same with a photo of a man[6]. In other words, they were being asked to identify what the ideal body shapes were for their own countries. The results are fascinating. Some of the European and Asian images would be regarded by experts as unhealthily underweight, with Italy and China having the thinnest ideals. In the male collection, the USA and Egypt had the strongest focus on defined abdominal muscles; Russia had the biggest shoulder and pectoral muscles. Take a look and see what you think.

> "In some East Asian countries, there's a trend to look Korean, dying hair pink, blonde, gold, etc, wearing special contact lenses to make eyes look bigger. Cosmetic surgery, including to change the shape of facial features, is very common and lots of Koreans – male and female – get cosmetic surgery vouchers for their 13th birthday."
> **Peggy, young adult, Malaysian**

Some communities do celebrate a bigger ideal. A 2011 report[7] in the US compared attitudes to weight in African-American and white teenagers aged 10–14. African-American girls were less likely to report weight issues than white girls and less likely to

---

5   www.scienceofpeople.com/perceptions-of-perfection-women/
6   www.scienceofpeople.com/perceptions-of-perfection-men/
7   www.ncbi.nlm.nih.gov/pmc/articles/PMC3138864/

suffer low self-esteem if overweight. (All studies like this show generalities: of course, many girls and boys of all colours can have problems with weight and self-esteem.) Nigeria is one example of a country where carrying plenty of weight can be a sign of wealth, health and beauty, though this may be changing.

 "I grew up in Britain, but I know from family and friends in Nigeria that being big used to be a sign of wealth because it showed you had enough money to eat all you want and not just being able to afford the minimum. But I don't think it's widely believed anymore and Nigerian celebrities are often skinny. Healthy food is getting more expensive than junk food so being slim shows you can afford to eat expensive food. I also think that a rise in type 2 diabetes has changed the attitude to fat. Nigerian tribes and groups vary massively, so this is only my observation from my own culture."

Paula, Nigerian heritage

And there are many other specific beauty ideals in different communities: women of the Pa Dong tribe in southeast Asia use rings to stretch their necks, a traditional mark of beauty; in China, there was a time when small feet in women were so prized that baby girls would have their feet bound to stop them growing; the Karo tribe in Ethiopia view scars as attractive in both men and women. Beauty is, as Plato said, in the eye of the beholder.

"In China, girls seem to be more aware of body shape compared to boys. Also, 'thanks' to social media like WeChat, fashion trends appear for very young teenagers. Girls bombard WeChat with pictures of their successful attempts at various trending looks. After I came to the UK, I noticed many boys worry about their physique and

saw it affect the social hierarchy in friend groups. Height also affects self-esteem for boys my age."

Alan, Chinese boy at a UK school

Young people growing up in a culture that's not their own can face extra challenges, as there may be conflict between what their family and community thinks is right and what their friends of other cultures aspire to. For example, say you're from an Indian ethnic background but you're growing up amongst mostly white friends: you can be torn between the ideals of your Asian and white communities.

"I was born in India to Punjabi parents and came to live in the UK at about 10-11 months. Later, I went to a girls' grammar school, 1,000 girls with two British Asian girls (including me) and one mixed-race girl who was one of my friends. Nearly all the English girls had a pretty healthy relationship with their bodies and no one was particularly overweight. Self-harming, anorexia, bulimia, did not seem common.

"I felt very different. My parents were very strict, traditional Hindus. My skirt had to be long, my hair long and plaited, my breasts squashed down. I had to wear looser clothes, nothing snug or close-fitting. No cleavage or bare skin. Being overweight for a girl in our community was not good, but boys could be and do as they wanted. Asian girls faced pressures to cover up so we didn't attract attention, shame our families, besmirch our honour. I remember the feeling of wanting to be 'normal' like the other girls in my grammar school, of having no hang ups about my body."

Savita, British Asian

SKIN COLOUR - IT'S ALL RELATIVE

Skin colour is part of body image. Unfortunately, there's often a perceived status angle: historically, being pale might indicate that you can afford to pay people to work outside for you. So, white women in Victorian Britain, for example, wanted to be pale and freckle-free, to  show they were ladies of leisure with staff to bring cooling drinks as they relaxed under a parasol. When rich Europeans travelled to Asia or Africa, they used to expect servants to wait on them and keep them cool out of the sun. So, pale skin for those people showed status.

 "In Punjab, light skin is considered far more attractive than dark. Coming back from holiday once, I remember my mum saying I had gone 'black', and for her that was not a good thing."
Savita, British Asian

In some darker-skinned cultures, such as India, being a paler shade of dark is still seen as desirable, with the skin-lightening industry worth many billions. The *Times of India* in 2018 had a piece[8] titled '8 ways you can achieve a lighter and flawless skin tone', which began, *'Everyone wants a flawless, beautiful and lighter skin tone... Wondering how to get fair skin? Try these effective lightening tips and get that lighter skin you can flaunt really soon.'* South Korea is another example of a country where skin-lightening is prized and people spend a lot of money on all sorts of products to achieve this.

....

8   https://timesofindia.indiatimes.com/life-style/beauty/want-a-lighter-skin-tone/articleshow/16736840.cms

Meanwhile, many pale people in Northern Europe or the US go to great lengths to get tanned-looking skin, from a bottle, tanning studio or lying in the sun and risking premature ageing and skin cancer. Maybe it's because being too pale is also linked to being unwell, and people want to look healthy, even though there's nothing healthier about a tanned skin. There can also be a status element here: you're tanned because you can afford to be. We know the risks of sunbathing, but many people ignore those risks for the sake of what they think looks great, even though a suntan fades quickly or is expensive to maintain.

CAN WE CHANGE SOCIETY AND THESE IDEALS?

When we catch ourselves aspiring to the body ideals in the media, we've been brain-washed by an industry that wants us to spend time, money and head-space changing something that is already brilliant: our body. But how can we fight back?

We can't change history but we can change the culture we live in. You are part of this change: you have power. With tiny steps, gestures and personal protests, we can change people's minds. We can speak out when people fat-shame or when we hear negative body talk. We can write letters to media outlets that focus too much on skinny or that pressure people to change how they look or advertise diet pills on health websites. We can change how people around us see body image and how highly they value health over appearance. That's what I'd like to do with this book. But we have to start with ourselves.

Changing minds always starts with our own. Charli Howard couldn't stand up to the modelling industry until she'd changed her own mind and believed that the industry standard wasn't right.

So, what can we do, each of us? If you do all the Body Boosts in this book, you're more than half way to having a better body image for yourself. Understand how your mind tricks you, how the images you see around you deceive, and choose to be wiser and stronger. If you can do that for yourself, you can spread that thinking amongst your friends and peers. And adults. Then you've changed society in some small way.

"I come from a background where women and girls might wear a hijab or headscarf. My mother and grandmother and many women in my family do this but I don't want to. My hair is one of my best features and I don't want to hide it. I don't like the way a headscarf feels on my head and I only wear one when I'm going to madrasah or to pray. Me and my friends like to talk about each other's hair and what we could do with it and if they couldn't see my hair I couldn't be in the conversation properly."
Shaniqua, 12

BODY BOOST

Look at the websites 'Perceptions of Perfection' for men and women mentioned at the end of this chapter. Do you prefer the 'ideal' images for the country you are from? If so, you've been influenced by what's around you. Remind yourself that these ideals are relative and see if you can create your own personal ideal of strength and health.

Summing up

There is no one perfect body shape: it's all fashion – much of it forced on us by big business wanting us to spend money. In many times and cultures, being curvy and big was a positive thing, signifying status, wealth, strength – and beauty. As for colour, some darker-skinned people want to become lighter and some lighter-skinned people want to be darker – the world is an illogical place!

Beauty is not skin-deep – it's soul-deep. Having a better body image starts with recognising that 'beauty' is relative and changeable. There's no absolute truth. Start to see yourself as just as valuable, human and 'real' as someone whose body happens to be a different shape.

Let's change minds, one mind at a time, starting with our own. Let's do this, because your brilliant body deserves it.

RESOURCES FOR THIS CHAPTER

<u>ONLINE</u>

Through history:

www.scienceofpeople.com/ideal-body-types-throughout-history/

Perceptions of Perfection:

when designers altered a man/woman to look 'ideal' for their country.
www.scienceofpeople.com/perceptions-of-perfection-men/ and
www.scienceofpeople.com/perceptions-of-perfection-women/

'Weight Misperceptions and Racial and Ethnic Disparities in Adolescent Female Body Mass Index':

www.hindawi.com/journals/jobe/2012/205393/

Colourism:

www.facebook.com/bbcthree/videos/10156087494760787/

<u>BOOKS</u>

<u>Fiction</u>

Beauty Sleep by Kathryn Evans – YA novel in which a girl wakes up in 2028 after being asleep for 40 years. Fascinating insight into beauty ideals as they are now, compared to how they were in the 1980s and how they might be a decade from now.

chapter *three*

INTERNET, SOCIAL MEDIA AND CELEBRITY CULTURE

 "A lot of people are obsessed by appearance because public figures focus on it so much and celebrities often alter their photos to look better. But it's not really their body if the photo has been altered!"

Nana Kwame, 14

I've mentioned that we compare ourselves to the people around us. Let's explore that.

All animals are programmed to fit in with their species or group: it's safer not to be different, so as to be accepted by the group. It's fine to stand out as the strongest or have the best coat or biggest antlers or brightest feathers, but not to have different features. In the animal kingdom that can often lead to being rejected. Rejection threatens survival.

Humans have those instincts, too, though being human also gives us the power not to reject, but to look beneath appearances to the person within.

But even when we are decent humans, valuing all humans whether they look like us or not, we are still comparing ourselves. Not necessarily negatively or positively (though often that, too), but just noticing and measuring, often unconsciously.

One illustration is how people mimic each other without meaning to. One person yawns and suddenly others do. One person grins and your smile muscles twitch. How we talk can change, too, depending on who we're with. We are constantly trying to fit in.

WHAT HAVE THE INTERNET, SOCIAL MEDIA AND CELEBRITY CULTURE GOT TO DO WITH COMPARISON?

Before television, magazines or the internet, people could really only compare themselves with people around them. They mostly saw people going about normal lives: no touched-up photos, clever lighting and fake images of beauty created by advertisers trying to sell something. They'd see many body shapes and have a good sense of 'normal'. No cosmetic surgery or clever ways for people to change how they looked, other than make-

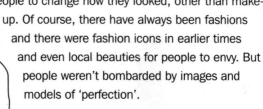

up. Of course, there have always been fashions and there were fashion icons in earlier times and even local beauties for people to envy. But people weren't bombarded by images and models of 'perfection'.

Along came newspapers, magazines and then television: our view was widened. We saw people of different appearances and were encouraged to admire people chosen to model whatever advertisers wanted us to buy. At first, images were illustrations, not photos, so the (usually male) artist could make them any shape he wanted. But in those days of a few TV channels and no internet, you'd still spend most of your life not looking at models, still surrounded by real people with varied appearances.

A constant stream of images

But now, with the amount of time so many of us spend online, it's virtually impossible not to be bombarded by images, usually very artificial, promoting a particular shape, one that we can't have unless we go to extreme lengths and costs. It has been estimated that by the time a girl reaches the age of 17, in a media-rich country, she will have seen 250,000 commercial messages, many telling her how she should look. Various studies into the content of these suggest that magazine or online materials aimed at girls are far more likely to have messages about beauty ideals than is the case for boys (though boys don't escape.)[9]

Also, the advertisers give us what they think we're interested in, based on our age, gender and what we just looked at, which are the three basic things they know about you.

---

9 www.healthyplace.com/eating-disorders/articles/eating-disorders-body-image-and-advertising

> "As a teenager, I devoured glossy magazines, torturing myself with painful aspirations. I never managed to process the knowledge that the images were highly artificial. They felt real to me and they made me feel inadequate. It didn't help that my family contains famous beauties and models."
>
> **Frances**

To illustrate this, I noticed that within hours of starting to research this book by putting 'body image' and 'teenage body image' into search engines, my social media and other feeds were full of adverts I'd never had before. Over the next two days, they were for, in order of quantity: #1 Diet pills #2 Weight loss surgery #3 Breast implants #4 Products with 'Bikini-body' in the description #5 Cosmetic surgery #6 Cellulite removal.

Notice that I'd only put in 'teenage body image'? They aren't interested in what I want to know, only what they want me to know. With the exception of yoga adverts, I saw nothing that promoted health and strength, only things to do with weight loss. Even the yoga adverts featured only thin women. I'm a middle-aged woman searching 'body image' so I must want to lose weight and improve my breasts? What a grotesque, undermining assumption! I actually don't want either of those things. I wouldn't mind having better hair, but don't tell the internet that, as I'm not that bothered.

Celebrity influence

Celebrity culture is now a vast industry and a way of selling everything from clothes, jewellery and perfume to cosmetic surgery, weight-loss pills and diets, many of which don't work and/or are dangerous. It almost certainly influences you in some way, even though you might not realise it and even if you try to rise above it.

> "Growing up has always been stressful but our parents never had the pressure of social media. I began to obsessively check my phone to keep up with my friends or to view the 'perfect' life and body of the newest Instagram model. Not only did this increase my anxiety, it harmed my sleep. The pressure increased as I saw people posting more pictures of their bodies, making me think I had to look like them. I started to pick things out that I hated about my body and cover up my insecurities. I never used to be self-conscious, but now I feel I have to look a certain way. Teenagers don't always realise that what they're seeing on a social media profile isn't an accurate representation of life."
>
> **Jemma, 16**

The figure is often quoted that only around 5 per cent of American women have the body shape currently pushed as ideal. A majority of girls and women say they're influenced by models in magazines and online.[10] Those pieces of information together illustrate the pressure to lose weight and aspire to a shape that isn't natural or possible for the vast majority. So, people may be tempted to resort to attempts that can be expensive, harmful and soul-destroying.

As for boys, they may be trying to bulk up when they haven't reached the developmental stage where that's physically possible. Muscles aren't simply the result of exercise: you need the correct adult hormones in your body for exercise to have that effect.

10 http://www.admedia.com/media-and-body-image.php

Or do you think you're able to look at all these images and not be influenced? Many people think that. If you look at many different-shaped models, perhaps, but if you're mostly seeing one particular shape, your brain can't avoid processing those shapes as 'normal'.

I have a question for you: have you ever looked at and laughed at one of those photos that shows a celebrity with a caption that highlights something designed to be negative? Perhaps the photo focuses on a roll of fat or streaked make-up, or some cosmetic procedure that had gone wrong?

Let's not do this. I know you might think, 'They deserve it – they're so focused on how perfect they are and it's great to see them brought down a bit.' But isn't that just adding to the pressure on everyone to be perfect? Didn't you just join the crowd of cruel people who focus on perfect appearance instead of brilliant actions and great minds? It's easy to fall into this trap but I think we can create a better world if we don't.

ADVERTISING AND TOYS ←

It's not just human beings, but toys and dolls. Barbie has long been criticised for having an unrealistic body shape and encouraging young girls to aspire to that. My Little Pony seems to me to have changed its shape from the 1990s to now, with a slimmer look as though it has a waist.

Many people have traced the changes in body shape of GI Joe, the action doll, from the 1960s to recent models. His huge sculpted muscles are far more evident in recent versions and the way he is portrayed on packaging reveals a greater focus on extreme muscle power. Take a look at the resources at the end of this chapter for more information.

Toy-makers often unnecessarily market certain products as 'for boys' or 'for girls', focusing on image and appearance. The UK's 'Let Toys Be Toys' campaign[11] tries to tackle this. If toys or packaging suggest that 'this is how a girl looks and behaves and this is how a boy does', children can worry whether they fit that narrow stereotype of boyness or girlness. Why not just feel free to wear what you want and look how you want?

---

11 http://lettoysbetoys.org.uk/

Toys and clothes have a lot to do with body image, as they are part of fitting in or standing out – part of how you see yourself.

ISN'T THE INTERNET A GOOD THING, TOO?

Yes! Many celebrities promote a fantastic body image message. And one of the great things about the internet is how messages spread widely. In fact, the internet and social media are what allowed the body positive message to spread and promote the use of curvy models. The Internet can be a force for good as well as bad.

 "Social media has helped me. There is much talk on social media about representation, or represent Asian, and seeing people on screen or in books who actually look like me. I didn't have this growing up, so I am glad my daughter will."
Shaheen

In the resources at the end of this chapter, you'll find examples of great role models, female and male. Most of these role models don't have as many followers as the more negative ones, but how about we start listening to them and thinking properly about what they're saying rather than blindly following people who've got rich media companies throwing money at them so that they can sell us things?

> *"Some celebrities do show a positive body message. For example, YouTubers joewoahy and Joey Graceffa are openly gay and encourage other people not to be shy about being LGB. Another YouTuber, Azzy, is supportive of people who don't like how they look and you would never catch her being rude about people who are either curvy or skinny."*
> **Shaniqua, 12**

If you spend time looking at images of these confident, bold, strong, beautiful men and women, it will start to change any negative feelings you might have about different body shapes.

BODY BOOST

Control your online environment: choose activities that are useful, creative or make you feel good – or all of those!

You have the choice of what you look at, so use it well. It will make a difference to how you feel and how you feel makes a difference to how you approach life.

SPECIFIC PROBLEMS WITH ONLINE CULTURE AND BODY IMAGE

Perfectionism

It seems[12] that more people are suffering from perfectionist behaviour now than ever. Perfectionism is the intense desire and need to live up to the ideals one has set oneself and the fear of not achieving those targets. If perfectionism just meant being ambitious to succeed, it wouldn't be a problem, but when it's an obsession and a fear, it becomes a problem in two ways: it leads to constant dissatisfaction and it can make people focus on unhelpful targets and beat themselves up about trivial imperfections or mistakes.

> "I think social media is a really negative influence and I'd like to ask people not to believe what they see there. The fact that models are always thin is a problem."
> **Stella, 15**

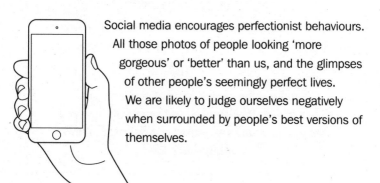

Social media encourages perfectionist behaviours. All those photos of people looking 'more gorgeous' or 'better' than us, and the glimpses of other people's seemingly perfect lives. We are likely to judge ourselves negatively when surrounded by people's best versions of themselves.

12 https://www.apa.org/pubs/journals/releases/bul-bul0000138.pdf

A study in 2017[13] suggested that increasing rates of perfectionist behaviour could be linked to rising mental illness in young people. There's no proof and there are other possible causes but perfectionism is strongly linked to anxiety, which is common in depression and anxiety disorders. Perfectionism feeds off the need to measure up to peers.

"It bothers me how people keep on about being thin. People are all sorts of shapes and not everyone is thin. Some people are still fatter than I am even though we mostly eat the same. I like to grow food to eat so maybe that helps and it mostly stops me having spots, too. I am not too bothered about how I look. Maybe it will be different if I have a boyfriend. I like boys but I like them just as people right now."

Anne, 13

Perfectionism can play a huge part in eating disorders, too. And since so much celebrity culture and media advertising is about thinness for girls and women and fat-free bodies for boys and men, you can see why a perfectionist personality can easily move from a fairly harmless wish to lose a bit of weight to a dangerous obsession with controlling appearance.

"I don't like thinking you have to buy special clothes with the brand name on them. It's usually heaps more expensive. Some of my friends think you have to have those things and they tell me I should but I don't see the point."

Anne, 13

....

13 https://www.theguardian.com/commentisfree/2018/jan/05/perfectionism-mental-health-millennial-social-media

*Celebrity culture encourages **perfectionism** in three ways:*

1. It showers us with examples of what we 'should' or could look like. It offers what look like targets, even when the images are so often touched up.

2. It gives us the opportunity to aspire to be more 'perfect', with products and tips and the celebrities talking about how they can help us.

3. It can make us feel ashamed if we're nothing like the models. We can easily become dissatisfied with ourselves.

Narcissism

A narcissist is focused entirely on themselves. It is an extreme version of selfishness. We can all be selfish sometimes. That's fine: we have to think of ourselves. But a narcissist rarely thinks about anyone else. It particularly applies to physical appearance. In fact, the word comes from an ancient Greek story, where Narcissus was so incredibly proud of his own beauty that he stared at his reflection for so long that he lost the will to live.

"I think it's a problem that most models are not a realistic shape because it sets unrealistic targets. It can also harm the models themselves."
Daniel, 14

*Celebrity culture encourages **narcissism** in three ways:*

1. It rewards appearance. We see people become rich and famous because of how they look.

2. It provides opportunities to be narcissistic, with expensive make-up, lighting, cosmetic procedures and the focus on selfies.

3. It makes focusing on appearance feel normal and desirable. It can seem that not focusing on appearance means there's something wrong with you.

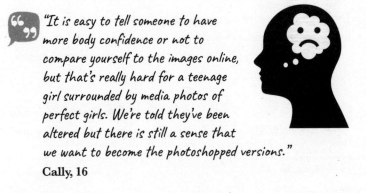

"It is easy to tell someone to have more body confidence or not to compare yourself to the images online, but that's really hard for a teenage girl surrounded by media photos of perfect girls. We're told they've been altered but there is still a sense that we want to become the photoshopped versions."

Cally, 16

Cosmetic surgery

In the US, cosmetic procedures are increasing[14] and they're becoming more widespread in other countries, too, in South Korea above all. People can have permanent implants put into breasts, buttocks, cheekbones, pretty much anywhere that fashion says we 'ought' to have a bit more flesh.

Such procedures aren't new. Back in the eighties and until her death in 2002, the ever-changing body of actress Lolo Ferrari was in the media spotlight. Ferrari had around 30 operations, mostly to increase her breast size, which eventually each contained three litres of surgical liquid and were so big she couldn't walk, lie down or breathe normally.

The increase in cosmetic surgery in recent years has happened partly because the surgery is now possible; partly because the online world has bombarded us with stories of what's possible and encouraged us to try it; and partly because of the human habit of often wanting more than we have.

There are no clear or consistent regulations about minimum ages for cosmetic procedures and there are too many surgeons who don't enquire deeply enough into someone's mental state before agreeing to go ahead.

 "The internet creates 'perfect figures' that everyone thinks are best. Models don't seem like real people to me: they are artificial and enhanced."
Charlie, 13

....

14 https://www.plasticsurgery.org/news/press-releases/new-statistics-reveal-the-shape-of-plastic-surgery

It's wonderful that medical advances have made it possible to solve distressing and disfiguring problems and to make life better for many people who previously would have had no choice, but I'm worrying about people trying to chase perfection through surgery. People believe that changing their body will cure their unhappiness or anxiety, and often it doesn't.

Who am I to say that someone shouldn't spend their money how they want? Thing is, I want people to be healthy and happy and I believe there are better ways to achieve that. I think we should help each other stand up against media messages that say, 'This is how beautiful people look. You could look like us if you did this diet, starved yourself, went to the gym every day, bought expensive face creams and had a surgical procedure or three.'

 "I think it's a problem that most female models are thinner than average and most male models are more muscled than average. It creates pressure and can cause depression and anxiety. I think people should be themselves."
Maria, 15

Temporary cosmetic procedures

Children's author, Fiona Dunbar, wrote a paper in 2013 called 'Girls and Body Image', tracing the role of the media in body image and eating disorders. In it, she talks about the rise in professional manicures and pedicures for three-year-olds. 'That's the sort of thing that robs a child of her childhood. What these three-year-olds are already learning is that girls and women aren't good enough the way they come: that they need fixing.'

"Plastic surgery is a rubbish idea. Everyone is beautiful."
Stella 15

In the few years since that paper, we've entered a world where teenage and young adult girls ask for lip-filler treatment for a birthday or other present. Lip-filler treatments are temporary, lasting a few weeks or months at the most, so, if you like the result you're likely to want it again. And again. And as well as lips, you can get other aspects of your facial shape changed – temporarily, expensively and riskily. You've all seen the pictures of what can happen when it goes wrong, as it's more likely to do if you try to get it done cheaply. These procedures tend to be unregulated (unlike physical surgery) and it's possible for someone to get a certificate after a single day of training.

There are online support groups for people considering cosmetic procedures, but often there's a hidden agenda and the person you're talking to might have something to gain from you going ahead with the procedure. Social media platforms are also full of adverts and discussions about these procedures and it's difficult or impossible to tell which are offering genuine independent and expert advice.

 "Most girls and women I talk to are not happy with their bodies, particularly their weight. This now extends to men, with the need to gain muscle. This is hardly surprising when you look at the culture we live in; products are advertised on photoshopped bodies, devoid of cellulite, stretch marks, hair and most of the things our bodies have. As a user of social media, it is virtually impossible to avoid fake body expectations. Even if you do not actively follow fashion/gym/ health/fitness accounts, they creep into your pages."
Charlotte, young adult

Apart from the obvious risks, who am I to say that having something like filler treatment is wrong, if you can afford it? I discussed this with a group of teenagers aged 12 to 17, and heard various opinions, but the large majority thought it a bad idea. A couple of them felt it was fine if it would make you happy and you could afford it but my question is: how would it make you happy in the long-term? Would you not then become even more obsessed by the shape of your lips (or whatever bit you've altered) and want it done again and again? Is this really a way of spending your money that's going to give you satisfaction? Would you not be *happier* finding a better direction for your time, talents and values?

If you are thinking about having any cosmetic procedures, I discuss this further on pages 276–8.

Facial contouring with make-up

The possibilities of changing our appearance with make-up are now vast, with the introduction of contouring make-up that allows people to alter the shape of their face in so many ways. This is something that has been promoted widely by celebrities online.

This type of make-up can really help people who have decided to cover up a mark or scar or anything that is stopping people seeing the person beneath. But for other people, who are trying to achieve a particular look for fashion reasons, I think there are some negatives to consider.

The cost, for a start: these things are not cheap! The time involved is huge: watch any of the video tutorials and you'll wonder how anyone manages to find this amount of time. Then there's the pressure of having to do it all the time –

because you might feel 'unattractive' on the days you didn't put full make-up on.

 "You only see people at their best on social media and it's impossible to be your best all the time."
Rachel, 14

It's worth remembering that the big advocates of facial contouring and lengthy make-up routines are people or companies with make-up to sell.

It's also worth realising that not everyone buys into this fashion. In South Korea, for example, which has the highest rates of cosmetic surgery procedures and an intense focus on 'perfection' through make-up and fillers – fuelled partly by the K-pop music scene – there's also a strong movement called Escape the Corset[15] which encourages people not to feel they have to do any of these appearance-changing behaviours. It's interesting that modern ideals are trapping women in just the same way as the actual corset used to in the days when we had to wear them if we wanted to fit beauty standards.

Filters and photo enhancement

Social media filters give us temptation and opportunity to change our public appearance, particularly when we take selfies. They – and all the other bits of software that allow people to touch up and digitally alter their photos – offer the chance to everyone to look flawless. You can alter the shape of your eyes or the colour of your skin, remove natural blemishes and even delete the appearance of all pores; you can have a smoother jaw, lusher hair, higher cheekbones, a different-shaped nose; you can

15 https://www.theguardian.com/world/2018/oct/26/escape-the-corset-south-korean-women-rebel-against-strict-beauty-standards

look more like your celebrity hero, with equally perfect skin and gorgeousness, just with a couple of minutes of fiddling with your phone. You'll naturally want to put that photo out there rather than the unfiltered one, won't you?

 "Filters on Snapchat often change minor details like slimming your face or altering your nose. I don't agree with this. It can definitely make people feel more insecure about 'imperfections' that no one else is actually noticing."
Daisy, 14

What's wrong with this? It doesn't cost us anything (apart from the phone, the data and sometimes the software) and it doesn't harm us, does it? One problem is that when we look at our real self in the mirror, we're likely to feel upset that we don't live up to our online image or that perfect selfie. We can start to judge ourselves even more and be even more negative about our appearance. Meanwhile, we see everyone else's 'flawless' images online and ourselves in the mirror, and are even more likely to want to enhance our own photos.

So, yes, this can harm us. It can harm our body image. When we meet people in real life, we suspect that they are surprised that we look so different from our photos. Of course, lots of people naturally look different from their photos but usually it's the other way around: our photos are more often unflattering and don't do us justice. If the filters just made us look like our real selves on a good day and with the best lighting, that would be fine: but they can alter us so much that they aren't really us.

"Most models in magazines are really skinny and have flat stomachs. This is not how people are but it makes you want to be like that."
Sasha, 15

These filters also encourage and enable young people – and often younger than the readers of this book – to look sexualised before they're really at that stage of development. How we look – or how we see ourselves – affects how we feel about ourselves.

Gym culture

For many celebrities, going to the gym is a big part of their image and how they keep in shape and many people want to copy this. The gym is where people bulk up and build muscle, or develop the ripped look that is one of today's ideals for men (and some women). It's also a way that people try to get thin. But is it dangerous?

 "The need for boys and girls to fit the tight perfect window of body image is more of a problem than ever. As a 16-year-old, I see this a lot: boys trying to fit a broad-shouldered, muscular ideal and girls trying to become thin like models. This mindset is extremely damaging: people miss meals, prioritising how they look over more important things."
Jack, 16

Of course, gyms are there to build fitness and strength, and that's good. But 'gym culture' becomes a problem when going to the gym is about appearance more than health and fitness. It becomes about eliminating fat or building certain muscle groups to achieve a particular look. So, just as a healthy diet should be about eating and enjoying the foods that are going to help your body work as well as possible, so should exercise be about having a brilliantly healthy and strong body, in the gym or anywhere. And it shouldn't be the only thing we spend time on: there are many other important parts of a balanced life and a brilliant body and mind.

Thing is, you can't have the ripped, muscled look without going to lengths that most people would regard as extreme and which are potentially dangerous. Obsession with losing fat and sculpting your body in a particular way brings a high risk of eating disorders. More on that in chapter nine. I've also written about Muscle Dysmorphic Disorder on pages 137–8.

Social media has fuelled gym culture, showing us muscled, toned and ripped models. We can't always tell when images have been digitally altered but we're encouraged to believe that if we just spend more time in the gym, or buy more protein or energy drinks or other supplements, we, too, could look as ripped as fashion brand Logan Paul, footballer Cristiano Ronaldo, superman actor Henry Cavill or fitness icon Kayla Itsines.

"There is a lot of pressure to lose weight, especially for women. Diet pills are advertised alongside smiling women; banners reading, 'I lost X amount of weight in X amount of time!' are plastered across the back of buses; people on social media constantly post 'thin-spo' (thinsperation) or 'fitspo' pictures, all of which promote a certain body type. And if someone does not have that body? Well, they're 'not taking care of themselves' or 'lazy.'"

Iona

One of the problems with some cult TV programmes aimed at young people is that the actors are often older than the characters they play. For example, Cory Monteith was 27 when he started playing the 16-year-old character in TV show, *Glee*. A 27-year-old will naturally be able to have bigger muscles than a teenage boy could, so he is setting an impossible standard.

It's not just about muscles, either. Cristiano Ronaldo also pays expensive attention to teeth, skin, face and eyebrows. And that's typical of pretty much any male fitness brand: it's the whole look and the whole look isn't cheap. So, we talk about them as 'fitness' icons but they aren't only that – it's all about the look.

This word 'ripped' describes a look that has so little body fat that muscles are more noticeable. Be aware that 'ripping' is a very unpleasant process that body-builders go through specifically to lose body fat. They know it's dangerous so they don't do it for long, just before a competition. So, being ripped isn't about strength, health or even how much muscle you've got: it's purely about how little fat is under your skin; purely appearance; purely the culture of body-building.

"*Three years ago, one friend started to look at his photos and complain how skinny and small he was. From then, he has been obsessed with bulking up by going to the gym a lot and drinking protein shakes. He has put on lots of muscle and looks very different but he still wants more muscle. Unfortunately, he now has a very weak back and is prone to injuries which could be a problem for the rest of his life.*"

Sam, 16

Gyms are useful places where many people enjoy getting fit. If you're under 16, you probably won't be able to join a gym, but your school might have one and you might have weights or other equipment at home. As long as you realise that you can get fit in lots of other ways that cost little or nothing, that's your choice. If you enjoy going to the gym and you feel you're making yourself fitter and stronger and healthier, go for it. But don't overdo it, don't become obsessed, and don't do it for looks more than health. If you think you're becoming obsessed, talk to someone about it. Obsessions start small but take over.

CHANGING CULTURES?

It's possible that screens have changed the way whole cultures view themselves. A fascinating study[16] was done on adolescent Fijian girls in 1998, three years after television was introduced to Fiji. There was a rise in disordered eating over the next years and interviewing showed a trend 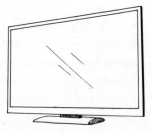 towards trying to copy the body shapes of women on television, moving away from traditional Fijian ideals of strength and fitness, rather than slimness.

That was pre-internet: now there are even more opportunities to see media images of beauty ideals. We are bombarded by photos of people whose appearance either fits the ideal (thin/toned/fit/sexualised) or has been altered by surgery, photo-enhancement, lighting, make-up or other trickery. The more we see those images, the more likely we are to think they're normal and to compare ourselves negatively with them.

....

16 Research by Anne E Becker MD, PhD Department of Social Medicine, Harvard Medical School and Adult Eating and Weight Disorders Program http://www.brown.uk.com/eatingdisorders/becker.pdf

THE EFFECT OF INTERNET PORNOGRAPHY

Pornography is defined as writing, pictures or film designed to sexually excite. Pornography is nothing new but internet porn is very different from the images that used to be in magazines. It is different in two main ways: first, it often portrays extreme violence including rape. Second, it is far easier for young people to access than magazines were.

Many people are worried about the possible serious negative effects of watching internet pornograph.

Although it's difficult to find accurate figures, we know that lots of young people do watch pornography. Sometimes it's accidental: research suggests that this happens quite often and it's easy to see how. Sometimes it's just natural curiosity about something that's forbidden or perhaps a friend shows you something. It can be difficult not to look at something your friends are looking at and you might even be teased for refusing to look. But sometimes people, including young people, can develop a serious habit of watching porn and it can dominate their lives.

WHAT ARE THE RISKS?

What we watch and read affects how we think. Seeing something once or twice may not make a difference (although there is a risk of seeing an image that disturbs you so much that you can't stop thinking about it), but if we keep seeing one type of message we are very likely to start thinking it's normal. One of the defining aspects of your stage of life is that you are (depending on your exact age as you're reading this) changing sexually, developing desires that you didn't have when you were younger, and your healthy sexual development and future relationships need you to have the best information, ideas, support and role models now. Internet porn does not provide that.

A lot of porn promotes these false messages:

🍀 That males and females have to look a certain way to be 'sexy' or attractive. The ideals in porn are very often:

For women: thin waist, large breasts and hips; long, glossy hair; shaved pubic area

For men: big; ripped or muscled with six-pack and obvious abs; shaved body

🍀 That sex involves force and domination, not consent

🍀 That violence is right

🍀 That women really want to be dominated and hurt

🍀 That this is what real men and women usually look like

🍀 That love, affection and respect play no part in sex

🍀 That natural is less attractive than artificial.

These are all dangerous and wrong. Good relationships are not built on that and if people think they are then they risk unhappy relationships. They may be dissatisfied with their partners, worry about sex and feel bad about their bodies.

It's easier to have a good relationship with someone if you have a good relationship with your body. Being intimate is more difficult if you hate your body or think it ought to look different from how it does. The images that dominate internet pornography make people think that their body has to be a certain way, has to look hairy only in the right places and has to be exactly the right shape.

Also remember that there's an art to creating porn: lighting, acting, setting are all expertly directed and practised. Even the 'perfect-looking' participants don't really look like that. If they were relaxing in private on the sofa or eating a meal, without make-up or lighting or holding their stomachs in and clenching their muscles, they would look much more like the rest of us.

It's fake, remember. It's cleverly designed to make the viewers feel a certain way. It's manipulative, with the power to brainwash people into thinking this is how humans are supposed to be when they have sex. It undermines the power of humans to love, support and respect each other.

BODY BOOST

Remember: most of what you see online is manipulated, enhanced, altered, edited. You're seeing what people want you to see. Make a poster about this. Some of the resources for this chapter might inspire you.

Summing up

The internet and social media have positive and negative influences on body image. Some celebrities promote an obsessive behaviour around difficult-to-achieve or unnatural looks, persuading us that a particular shape is the right one and often advertising expensive ways of trying to obtain this. But some people have stood up to this negative culture and are promoting a more natural range of body shapes and a healthier way of life which allows us to respect and enjoy who we are.

People of all ages are influenced by what we see and read and if we see and read one particular message or set of messages over another we can easily believe that this is normal, that this is how the world is. We will be healthier and feel better about ourselves if we keep our minds open to a variety of ideas and images and realise that what we see online is not the whole picture.

RESOURCES FOR THIS CHAPTER

ONLINE

Statistics on body image and the media:
www.admedia.com/media-and-body-image.php

Teen Health and The Media:
https://depts.washington.edu/thmedia/view.
cgi?page=fastfacts&section=bodyimage

The UK Mental Health Foundation successfully argued, in a letter to the Advertising Standards Authority in 2018, that adverts during ITV's *Love Island* 'painted a false picture of perfection' and 'exacerbated young people's insecurities':
www.mentalhealth.org.uk/news/our-letter-expressing-concern-about-cosmetic-surgery-advertising-love-island-itv

Social media and eating disorders: www.eatingdisorderhope.com/blog/social-media-cause-eating-disorders-children

'Teenagers blame social media for anxiety over body image':
www.thetimes.co.uk/article/teenagers-blame-social-media-for-anxiety-over-body-image-x7cvgcOwp

'Body image – film and TV' from MediaSmarts '... watching a ten-minute segment of [*Friends*] had a negative effect on how satisfied young women were with their appearance.':
http://mediasmarts.ca/body-image/body-image-film-and-tv

'Not everyone's as ripped as Ken – why these toys need a body image makeover': https://everydayfeminism.com/2016/06/boys-and-body-image/

Body image and toys – Barbie and GI Joe: http://mediasmarts.ca/body-image/body-image-toys

Very Well Family:
www.verywellfamily.com/media-and-teens-body-image-2611245

A sixth-former, Evie, talks about body image, social media and expectations:
https://parentzone.org.uk/article/%E2%80%98nobody-should-make-you-feel-bad-about-your-decisions%E2%80%99

Model Charli Howard's post against fashion's insistence on thinness went viral in 2015:
www.elle.com/fashion/news/a31254/charli-howard-open-letter/

Positive role models online:

Dina Torkia on fashion and empowerment for Muslim women:
www.dinatorkia.co.uk/

Chidera Eggerue, The Slumflower, on body positivity and feminism. 'I never got the opportunity to celebrate my teenage body because I was too busy picking it apart and condemning it, even though it was doing its best.' www.theslumflower.com/

Jameela Jamil campaigns against air-brushing and photo-shopping:
www.youtube.com/watch?time_continue=764&v=BXzO0z6fmhl

BOOKS

Fiction

Butter by Erin Lange – hard-hitting (and clever) story of a very overweight boy who decides to eat himself to death online, creating a website and building a media presence.

Beauty Sleep by Kathryn Evans – YA novel in which a girl wakes up in 2028 after being asleep for 40 years. Portrays social media as even more intrusive and image focused than today.

chapter four

ADOLESCENCE AND PUBERTY

Adolescence is a physical stage, when your body and brain go through major changes. You are transitioning from child to adult male or female and your body will make this happen without you doing or thinking anything about it.

 "When I was younger, I didn't really think about my physical appearance but as I got older and my physical appearance started to change then it really began to bother me."
Ninnah, 14

Chapter five covers gender questioning, which can hugely affect body image. Here, I'm talking about biological changes that turn a boy or girl into a man or woman, based around the different range and balance of hormones of each sex.

It's important to remember that a woman who is more curvy is neither more nor less a woman than one with fewer curves. Your curviness does not affect your femaleness. A man who is more muscular or has more facial hair than some other men is biologically no more or less a man. Your hairiness and muscliness do not affect your maleness. In both cases, there is a vast range of 'normal' shapes and sizes of each body part.

BODY BOOSTS

Adolescence is not a race: everyone gets there at different speeds. But everyone does get there. Look at the students two years above and two years below you – such a short time, so much difference!

→ WHAT PHYSICAL CHANGES CAN YOU EXPECT?

These changes may not happen in this order.

Girls

Changes can start as early as eight years old but more usually later, any time through teenage years.

♀ Growing taller – a 'growth spurt' – and changing body shape such as hips widening, less fat on the stomach and more on hips and breasts.

♀ Growth of pubic and underarm hair.

♀ Starting periods – the usual age is 11–14 but between 9 and 16 is medically normal. If periods haven't started by 16, it's worth seeing a doctor but there may be nothing wrong. Periods can be very irregular.

♀ Developing breasts – there's enormous variation, and thinking that you're too small or too big are common anxieties.

> "In India, I grew up amongst friends who were much more affluent and it caused huge problems. I had new uniforms only every 4–5 years so, when my top was too short, we attached a piece to it. My parents weren't highly educated or socially aware. My mum wouldn't (and couldn't afford to) buy me sanitary napkins and for almost a year I suffered using cloths in school, which gave me the worst school cred. My mum didn't think bras were good (and they cost money we didn't have) so I didn't get bras for a long time. So, my breasts sagged long before I was 25 and that still causes me enormous body image self-doubt."
>
> **Selvi**

Boys

Changes for boys usually start later than for girls, typically around age 11 or 12 but can be earlier or later, and the medically 'normal' age range for noticeable signs would be 9–14.

♂ Growing taller and changing shape. The growth spurt usually happens later for boys than girls, typically at around 12–13.

♂ Growth of pubic and other body hair, and facial hair.

♂ Growth of penis and testicles. Erections with ejaculation, including during sleep.

♂ Voice deepening.

♂ In much older teenagers, muscle-building becomes possible, but for younger teenagers exercise only strengthens but does not bulk up muscles.

At the end of this chapter there are resources to give you more detail.

"My body and face have changed and got bigger during secondary school but I'm very happy with that. I have a very positive body image. I stand out amongst my peers because I'm taller and bigger. When someone made a comment about my looks, it didn't faze me."

Stella, 15

HOW DO TEENAGE BODY CHANGES AFFECT YOUR BODY IMAGE?

Your body image has developed over the first ten years of your life and you enter your teenage years with certain preconceptions of what you look like compared to others. And then, often quite quickly, so many things change inside you and outside you and all around you that this can be very challenging.

BODY BOOST

Every time you notice one of your adolescent body changes, make your mind view it positively, with thoughts such as 'This is my body doing what it's meant to do'; 'Isn't nature amazing?'

Let's see how this can affect body image and your mental picture of yourself. There are three main things to think about and they are all connected:

🌱 How slowly or quickly you're changing compared to your peers

🌱 Self-consciousness

🌱 Whether you *like* these changes.

Slow or fast?

You could be among the first or the last in your group to start puberty and both can make you feel distressed and self-conscious. You might be teased or bullied and even casual comments can make you feel different. Since these changes take place over several years, this can dominate your feelings about yourself for some time.

"I don't believe school uniform helps with body image. I think everyone should be able to come to school in what you feel comfortable with and what makes you you. No one should feel like they have to hide away because they think they'll be judged. It all comes down to confidence."
Aquilat, 14

As you already know, comparing ourselves with people around us is what humans naturally do. If you notice that others are physically changing faster or more slowly than you, it can make you feel that you stand out.

Girls can feel very distressed by breast development: some might be distressed because they think their breasts are too big and others because they're hardly growing at all. Both those situations can cause teasing from boys and from girls. Since the so-called 'ideal' is currently for big breasts, and most girls will not have big breasts – and certainly not if they have a very small waist – the 'ideal' is unattainable. That's hard.

Periods starting early can also be really difficult. Add the fact that in some cultures when a girl starts her periods she starts wearing a headscarf or dressing differently and you have a very public display of something that feels private. In some cultures, having your period is seen as making you 'unclean' and requiring you to hide away.

For boys, the visible signs of becoming a man can be just as difficult to manage: whether your facial hair is growing or not, whether you have developed muscles, whether your voice has broken, having wet dreams and erections, and whether you think your penis is larger or smaller than average: all these can make you self-conscious, particularly if they are happening earlier or later than for your peers.

Feeling self-conscious

One teenage brain difference concerns self-consciousness. (This is about 'typical' behaviour, which means that not everyone will experience it, but that very many do.) When teenagers think about or experience a socially embarrassing situation, the areas of the brain that activate during embarrassment tend to do so more than other age groups. And we observe teenagers finding some things more embarrassing than adults tend to.

 "When I was younger I wished I had straight hair but now I love my hair. And I used to hate my nose but now I don't care."
Daisy, 14

So, the chances of you feeling really self-conscious are high. You may feel that everyone is looking at you and judging you. Sometimes they are, but often they are not. And people will tend to forget quickly, but you're still assuming they're thinking about you. It's normal for us to feel people are watching us, but it's often more a problem for your age group than others.

Teasing isn't pleasant at any age, but teasing about physical appearance at a time when you're biologically feeling more self-conscious *and* your appearance is changing (sometimes in ways you might not like) becomes a recipe for possible distress.

Loving or hating the changes?

People feel differently about the changes that are happening (or
not happening) for many reasons:

🍂 Role models in their family and community – some are more
   open or supportive than others; some parents are more at
   ease with their own body shape than others

🍂 How they already feel about their body

🍂 How they feel about their gender

🍂 How self-conscious they are

🍂 Their friendship group

🍂 The education they've had at school and home about
   body changes

🍂 Their general mood and level of happiness.

(NOT) BEING IN CONTROL

I think most people want control over their lives and bodies.
Feeling that we don't have control is one of the main factors in
stress-related illnesses for any age. But teenagers are in a special
position: often you *want* more control but you're not allowed it.
Younger children may not mind so much and adults tend to be

able to make their own rules for at least most parts of their lives. But for you, adults make rules and your body seems to be doing its own thing.

This is one reason why eating disorders often start during teenage years (though they can start earlier or later, too). You can't control so much of your life and you may think you can control body shape by restricting food or over-exercising. In the end, eating disorders will control you, rather than you controlling them, but it's this desire for control as your body changes in ways you don't like that can trigger the process.

Eating disorders are such an important part of any discussion about body image, so they have a whole chapter to themselves (see page 161). I just wanted to mention it here because it's so often during adolescence that eating disorders begin. And there's evidence that severe body dissatisfaction during teenage years is a strong predictor of eating disorders[17], so building positive body image at your age is really important.

BODY BOOST

Emotions all over the place? It's OK!
When strong feelings creep up on you, avoid hurting yourself or others by distracting yourself: go for a run, take five deep breaths, count backwards from 99 in threes, punch a pillow, dance to loud music, walk round the block, leave the room with a calm shell hiding your feelings. Feelings change.

17 Voelker et al 2015

Summing up

Understanding that the physical changes you're going through are normal and positive is a huge start to feeling better about those changes. Teenagers are not children: you are on your way to becoming an adult, with adult male or female shapes. Those changes will happen at their own speed, sometimes early and quickly, sometimes later and more slowly.

Because these changes happen at a time when everything around you is changing and you're working out who you are and where you fit, teenage body changes can be stressful and frustrating and make you feel particularly self-conscious and dissatisfied. Comments from other people can be really wounding.

These physical changes and the discomfort that can accompany them will pass. You will reach your adult size and this will soon be your 'new normal'. Be kind to yourself and your friends and if you need support or are worried about anything to do with your body changes, ask a trusted adult.

RESOURCES FOR THIS CHAPTER

ONLINE

Kids Health: https://kidshealth.org/en/teens/puberty.html

Young Minds (UK): https://youngminds.org.uk/

My website: www.nicolamorgan.com

A breathing/relaxation exercise. Free audio on my website (search 'relaxation audio' on www.nicolamorgan.com) or Google 'belly-breathing'.

For girls:

https://teens.webmd.com/features/puberty-changing-body#1

Agnes for Girls: https://agnesforgirls.com/

For boys:

http://www.pamf.org/teen/health/puberty/physicalchanges.html

BOOKS

Fiction

Splash by Charli Howard – Molly excels at swimming but a chance remark from a friend about her size alters her focus. Friendships crumble as everyone is changing physically and mentally, but can they – and Molly's self-esteem – endure?

Blubber by Judy Blume – when her friend is teased for being overweight, Jill joins in. Only when she's bullied herself does she learn empathy.

Catalyst by Laurie Halse Anderson – a devastating story of perfectionism and what happens when a perfect life starts to unravel. For older teenagers.

Non-fiction

Blame My Brain – The Amazing Teenage Brain Revealed by Nicola Morgan

Positively Teenage by Nicola Morgan

Notes on Being Teenage by Rosalind Jana

Sex, Puberty and All That Stuff by Jacqui Bailey

A– Z of Growing Up, Puberty and Sex by Lesley De Meza and Stephen De Silva

Girl Files: All About Puberty and Growing Up by Jacqui Bailey

Boy Files: Puberty, Growing Up and All that Stuff by Alex Hooper-Hodson

chapter *five*

GENDER IDENTITY

When a baby is born, the first thing most people ask is 'Boy or girl?' The baby grows up surrounded by people who relate to that child as either male or female. Although many people try to treat babies and children the same, regardless of their sex, others don't; and even when we try, it's hard to be entirely gender-neutral. We are surrounded by society's expectations of how men and women are 'supposed' to look, dress and behave. Those are deep-rooted cultural behaviours and often make people assume what someone's gender is.

 "I think there's a way boys or girls are expected to dress. I personally think anyone should be able to wear anything because it's literally a piece of fabric sewn together to be put on your person."
Rachel, 14

THE LANGUAGE OF GENDER

Before I explain what body image has to do with this, let's discuss some terms that are commonly used when we discuss gender. The language and ideas surrounding this are changing quickly and not everyone agrees with some of the terms and meanings. I've done my best to find explanations that are inclusive and helpful, and I've asked people with personal experience of being gender questioning, but you might find better ways to define them. There are also other terms that people use, but these are starting points so you know what I mean when I use them. You will find some resources at the end of the chapter that will allow you to explore the terms even more and find definitions that work for you.

BODY BOOST

Build a list of people who accept you and care about you. That list can start with one person but will grow. Tell them how much you need them and how much their support helps you.

COMMON TERMS

Sex or gender? Sex is biological, signposted first by the reproductive organs a person has, as well as other biological characteristics, such as hormones and chromosomes. Gender is more complicated; there are lots of ideas about what it is and these ideas vary between cultures. It is, in short, how a person sees themselves in terms of male and female roles, behaviours and feelings.

Biological sex or assigned gender When a baby is born, it is assigned as male or female depending on visible sex characteristics. Assigned gender is the gender given to the baby based on their assigned biological sex.

Gender identity This is the gender people feel they are and is their personal experience; it might be different from their assigned gender. So, identity is about how you feel; it is your personal experience, which only you can know.

Gender expression This is how people express or *show* their gender identity. So, expression is about how you present your identity to other people. There is no wrong way to do this.

 "I and many other trans people would feel so much more comfortable in our skins if we didn't have to conform to binary gender appearances. I'm truly at the happiest with my body when I can mix and match elements of all genders, creating an identity for myself that is not one or the other. Our bodies are our own to play with, and one day, I hope society can view beyond gender to allow individuals to present as they wish."
Zan, young adult, F to non-binary

Gender dysphoria A medical term describing the potentially huge distress that some people experience as a result of feeling a different gender to the one they were assigned. The dysphoria can be felt bodily or socially, or both, or not at all.

Cisgender or Cis When a child who was assigned as a boy grows up identifying as a man, or a child who was assigned as a girl grows up identifying as a woman, that person is cisgender. A cisgender person identifies as the gender they were assigned at birth.

Transgender or trans People who do not identify with the gender they were assigned at birth. They may or may not choose to have medical or surgical treatment to help them live with a gender identity they feel comfortable with.

Transitioning When someone changes their gender role and expression to one that matches how they feel and identify, so they can live full-time according to their gender. This can range from life changes, such as dressing and behaviour (social transition), to medical changes, such as taking hormones and having various surgeries (medical transition).

Non-binary Someone who has a gender identity that is not exclusively male or female.

"As a teenager, before I understood how I felt about my body, I wanted breasts, long luscious hair and to feel comfortable in pink like my female peers. Later, those curves held a neon sign over my head, shouting that I was a woman. But I am not."
Zan, young adult, F to non-binary

Gender fluid Someone who sometimes identifies as female and sometimes male – or neither.

FtM and MtF These terms stand for 'female to male' and 'male to female', to describe people who have transitioned from the gender they were assigned at birth.

GENDER AND YOUR HORMONES

It's often how a person looks that first makes other people judge whether they are male or female. A baby's face, hair, hands and feet give no clues about sex. At first, the only visible differences are in the genitals, invisible to most people. Clothes can either emphasise or disguise a child's sex and many parents make a conscious decision to do one or the other.

But as babies become children and then teenagers, physical differences between boys and girls become more obvious. From puberty, this is much more obvious.

"I was assigned female and as a child, I could run free, skateboard and jump off sheds. My body didn't feel different. Being given a bra was the start of all the things that separated me from other girls. I tried to hide my feelings, to fit in with girl stereotypes, but I never wanted my breasts. I went to doctors multiple times, complaining my back hurt, as I heard they gave surgery to reduce breasts if they were painful."

Louis, young adult, FtM trans

These changes happen when the brain triggers the start of puberty and different chemicals (hormones) are released into the body. For males, the main hormone is testosterone and for females, progesterone and oestrogen. These hormones produce all the effects mentioned on pages 96–7. If nothing happens to block these hormones, then this will generally happen, regardless of any surgery or counselling for gender reassignment. So, when young people discuss transitioning with their doctors, hormone blocking can stop or delay these hormonal changes, to give a chance for lots of important and detailed discussion before any permanent steps. Then it is possible – which should be under strict medical supervision and after lots of consultation about the options – to replace the hormones with the ones for the gender the person is transitioning to. Later, some people will also choose gender reassignment surgery. However, some people, and particularly young people, will choose not to take any medical steps at all, just changing pronouns, clothes, hairstyle, until they decide what else they might want to do.

WHAT ABOUT 'INTER-SEX'?

A small number of babies have genitals which make it hard for doctors to assign their sex. And a few babies are born with normal genitals for a boy or girl, but later turn out not to have matching internal reproductive organs or to have a different chromosome structure from typical males or females or release different hormones from what is expected from their assumed sex. These people are 'intersex'. It's hard to know how common this is, partly because there are so many different intersex variations, but some estimates say that in the US 1 in every 1,500–2,000 babies are born requiring a specialist opinion about sex.

BODY BOOST

Find a way to describe simply and clearly who you are and how you feel, so that you can explain to someone if you want to. This might take some time but it is worth finding the words.

In the old days, when presented with a baby whose genitals made it difficult to decide the sex, doctors and parents would make a decision and the child would be raised as one or the other. Sometimes, surgery was carried out to make the baby look more like the sex they'd been assigned. Nowadays, more people believe that it's better to wait till the individual is old enough to know what gender they identify with before any interventions are considered. Each situation is different, both physically and emotionally, and each individual needs respect, expert knowledge and understanding. And very often no surgical or other intervention will be chosen, with the individual growing up and living a fulfilled life identifying with whatever gender they do.

WHAT HAS GENDER QUESTIONING GOT TO DO WITH BODY IMAGE?

Some gender-questioning people don't struggle with body image and we shouldn't assume that this is a problem for everyone. But for many, it's extremely important.

If you've grown up comfortable with your assigned gender, you will probably feel quite positive about becoming more visibly female or male in appearance. But if you're uncomfortable with the girl/boy label you've grown up with, when your body starts changing to become more like the gender that feels wrong for you, this can be extremely upsetting and overwhelming.

Adolescence

The bodies of boy and girl children are similar when they have clothes on, but the bodies of typical boy and girl teenagers and adults are usually very different from each other (although lots of cisgender women have small breasts and hips and lots of cisgender men don't have deep voices or lots of facial hair).

So, while younger children can feel uncomfortable in their body, puberty and adolescence bring a far greater chance of feeling really distressed, and this is when 'dysphoria' might be triggered. A younger child can more easily dress, play and behave in ways that are typical for the gender they identify; but once the body starts to change dramatically, it can be difficult or impossible to 'pass' as that gender if that's what the person wishes to do. (Many trans people are confident about being out as trans and don't wish to pass as their identified gender.)

> *"I wanted to have short hair, wear men's clothes. But I got a job on a bar where I learned if I wore make-up people would accept me; if I had long hair and a cleavage, they'd like me even more. But were these real friends? No. And they aren't the friends you really need."*
> **Louis, young adult, FtM trans**

Many (but by no means all) trans people talk about problems with body image as being dominant in their lives. They are also at higher risk of disordered eating and eating disorders[18]. Eating disorders have complex causes, but negative body image is often part of the picture. When you are distressed by the body you have, restricting food or exercising in specific ways are common (but risky) behaviours to try to alter and control a body that is not doing what you want it to do.

If you are experiencing this disconnection between your body and your gender identity, you'll know better than anyone but if, like me, you're just trying to understand how a trans person might feel, the best way to begin to feel real empathy is to read the lived experiences of trans people. But remember: every experience is different so hearing a few stories doesn't tell us

---

18 www.teenvogue.com/story/transgender-youth-eating-disorders

everything and every experience is valid, so, if you don't read your own experience in the stories you find, this does not mean that somehow your experience isn't real or right.

It's also important to realise that many trans people have a positive body image. There are many different ways of experiencing the life, body and mind one has.

"I'm sixteen and a half now, and I've been out as a trans male for about three years. I feel like my body shouldn't be the body I'm in. I know I'd be more comfortable and feel like myself if I had the body I feel I should have. Being referred to as a guy feels natural and normal. Puberty was hard, as curves start coming through, and people who are born male have their voice deepen, so a lot of people refer to me as a female because of my voice. What helped me most was meeting some trans people and realising that's what I had been feeling, but not being able to put a name to."

Nicholas, trans FtM

WORKING OUT WHO YOU ARE

Everyone is different and there are many ways of experiencing gender. For some people (usually cisgender people) their gender feels obvious and uncomplicated, but for others it can take a long time to work out exactly who they are. If you are questioning your gender or feeling uncomfortable with the 'girl or boy' roles, labels and attitudes around you, finding your identity while you're a teenager can be very difficult and require help.

"I haven't fully transitioned yet but I believe it'll be incredible for my self-confidence. But once I started going out and presenting as a male it felt natural, even if at first I was self-conscious about it."
Nicholas, trans FtM

 Sometimes feelings of dysphoria are temporary: it's perfectly possible to have a period of doubt and confusion and to end up identifying as the gender you were assigned. In fact, I've heard psychotherapists say that almost everyone questions aspects of their gender at some point.

But sometimes the discomfort remains strong and permanent. The support people get from those close to them and the experts who can help them decide how, when and whether to transition will make a big difference to how quickly and easily they find a positive state of mind and body.

Unfortunately, rates of mental illness are high amongst trans people[19] so it's really important to do everything you can to access the help available.

 "It can be hard to look different from what's typical for your gender but in our school you wouldn't be judged or targeted for this. It depends on your environment."
Daisy, 14

Luckily, there are lots of websites to help, and role models of various gender identities to think about and to help you find your way through it so that you can feel more comfortable in your body. Lots of people have been through this already and their experiences can help you greatly.

....

19 www.psychologytoday.com/us/blog/the-truth-about-exerci se-addiction/201612/why-transgender-people-experience-more-mental-health

Take as much time as you need to work out who you are and what you need. Be ready to listen and reflect and think.

MISGENDERING

The term 'misgendered' refers to when someone else mistakes the gender of that individual in some way. If the trans person feels that this was because of bodily appearance (as opposed to, for example, clothing), it's possible this could create distress about a particular body area.

Cisgender people can be misgendered, too. Lots of cis women have male facial features and small breasts and hips; lots of cis men have a curvier shape, including breasts. But for many trans people, being misgendered attacks the heart of who they are and hits them in the place where they most lack self-esteem and feel most vulnerable.

BODY BOOST

Is there someone you look up to? It could be someone in the trans community or not; it could be someone you know personally or someone you've never met. What would they say to you right now? Be that voice.

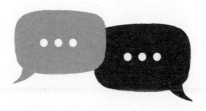

→ THE GOOD NEWS

Although the stages of transitioning are very often hard, when trans people receive the support they need and as they go further through the stages of their journey, they typically report better body satisfaction, resilience and self-understanding. When trans people are satisfied with their bodies and feel that they can pass as their experienced gender in social situations (if they want to), and feel confident in who they are, they can have a better quality of life and higher self-esteem.[20]

There's so much more help around nowadays and a greater acceptance of all the different expressions of gender. You'll find communities and groups, websites and blogs, videos and support, to help you find your way through, including some in the resources for this chapter.

BODY BOOST

Talk to someone. Talking helps. It could be a friend, parent, teacher, or someone from an online organisation that specialises in trans issues, but do get help. Help is out there.

20 Journal of Sexual Med 2016;13:1778e1786

Summing up

Although anyone can have a negative body image and low self-worth surrounding their appearance, and although many trans people are confident in their bodies, trans people or people questioning their gender or transitioning from one to another are at high risk of negative self-image and low self-esteem. However, in many societies today, there are new support systems and greater acceptance of gender diversity. You can now have a voice and be heard and you can come to respect and love the body you have and all it can do for you.

RESOURCES FOR THIS CHAPTER

Note that there are different views – and sometimes heated arguments – about how best to help young people who are questioning their gender, particularly in relation to the age at which medical treatment should start and the counselling that should happen first. Some organisations recommend a more 'wait and see' approach than others. There is also not yet enough research into some medical interventions. Do get as much help and support as you need from a variety of experts and discuss fully with people you trust, ideally more than one person. Remember that everyone is different and what worked for one individual may not be right for you.

ONLINE

Gender Spectrum: www.genderspectrum.org and www.genderspectrum.org/explore-topics/teens/#more-347

Young Stonewall – for all LGBTQ+ young people and with a section on gender here: www.youngstonewall.org.uk/lgbtq-info/gender-identity

Mermaids – specifically for gender-diverse young people: www.mermaidsuk.org.uk

The It Gets Better Project: https://itgetsbetter.org/

NHS (UK) on gender dysphoria: www.nhs.uk/conditions/gender-dysphoria/symptoms/

Growth Myndset gives insight into transgender thinking: www.growthmyndset.ca/blog/2018/3/31/avery-wing-inside-the-transgender-mind-trans-body-image-and-self-confidence

A US study researching body image in young trans people: https://www.sciencedirect.com/science/article/abs/pii/S1740144516302236

Eating Disorder Hope looks at a range of experiences: www.eatingdisorderhope.com/blog/the-transgender-look-body-imageidentity-and-eating-disorders-within-the-community

BOOKS

Be aware that stories have a particular power to trigger emotion. That's one of the wonderful things about them but, if you're feeling vulnerable, it's helpful to be warned so that you can make an informed choice about whether to read them.

Fiction

George by Alex Gino – "When people look at George they think they see a boy. But she knows she's not a boy. She knows she's a girl." George needs not only to become Charlotte but find a way to tell everyone.

If I Was Your Girl by Meredith Russo – Amanda has started a new school and is falling in love with Grant. But Grant doesn't know that Amanda used to be Andrew.

The Art of Being Normal by Lisa Williamson – David is an outsider, teased as such, but is struggling with his secret gender identity.

Non-fiction

Trans Mission – my quest to a beard by Alex Bertie – the memoir of a young man assigned female at birth.

What is Gender? How does it define us? And other big questions by Juno Dawson

Trans Global – The History of Transgender Around the World by Honor Head

chapter
six

SEXUALITY

SEXUAL ORIENTATION AND BODY IMAGE

Gender refers to how you feel about *yourself* and sexuality refers to who you are attracted to sexually or romantically. There are many different ways people define their sexuality, not only heterosexual (attracted to a different sex from your own) and homosexual (attracted to the same sex) or bisexual (attracted to both males and females). You can't choose who to be attracted to: it's just how you are. You can, however, choose how to express your sexuality and when to tell people. To 'express' your sexuality means the way you decide to show your sexuality and includes which codes you might follow, such as dress, hair and other outward markers of your inner self.

"In the LGBT media, you don't see common body shapes with cellulite, normal breasts, etc. You hardly ever see someone that hasn't got a six pack in the media."
Tom, young adult

How might body image be different for homosexual or bisexual people compared to how it is for people who are heterosexual? Remember first that it's different for everyone and, more than ever, what I'm going to say is about common feelings, not rules. If your own experience isn't reflected here, it does not mean it isn't valid. Also note that there isn't a lot of research on this yet and more research might bring different answers.

Body image *seems to be* – from people I've talked to and from people I've seen discussing this online, as well as from the research – a bigger or more common problem for gay men than straight men[21]. Gay and bisexual men have a high rate[22] of eating disorders, which doesn't prove worse body image, but the two often go together. Men in general often aspire to be lean and muscular[23], but studies suggest that gay men may more often be more dissatisfied when they don't have this shape. It may sound like a stereotype – gay men being ripped, having great fashion sense and taking a lot of care over their appearance – but many gay men do aim for this ideal.

BODY BOOST

Read a positive story by someone who has dealt with some of the same things as you: start with the It Gets Better Project website for inspiring stories. (The link is at the end of this chapter.)

21 https://www.bbc.co.uk/bbcthree/article/d9d886e1-b65c-40b3-8e3c-ad0f41aa1ea7

22 https://www.sciencedaily.com/releases/2007/04/070413160923.htm

23 http://psycnet.apa.org/record/2007-00915-002

Online channels and platforms aimed at gay men are dominated by images of super-toned, gym-sculpted, ripped models and those are the people who seem to get all the attention. Some young gay people pointed out to me that the images of gay men in the media are very non-diverse, with almost everyone being toned and thin, even amongst people who aren't professional models.

> *"Within the gay male community there are 'Tribes' which describe the look a person is conforming to. So, as well as the media constantly pressuring men to look as toned as possible, in the gay community there are also these boxes to fit into."*
>
> **Tom, young adult**

It can be terribly easy for a gay teenage boy to feel that that's the way he *must* try to look. But a teenage boy doesn't yet have enough of the right hormones to achieve that muscled look. This can create extreme dissatisfaction, which can become obsessive and lead to eating disorders and other negative behaviours and harmful ways of thinking.

The opposite is more often the case for gay women, with less body dissatisfaction than heterosexual women[24]. It seems that lesbian women on average may also have a larger ideal size than heterosexual women. This could be partly because they often reject the usual media ideals which tend to be dominated by male views of what women should look like. Since lesbian women don't feel the need to attract men and since feminism encourages them not to conform to thin ideals, they may be more able to set their own standards. And that can mean they don't

....

24 https://www.sciencedirect.com/science/article/abs/pii/S1740144513000715

have such a thin ideal. But some research contradicts that and the picture isn't at all clear. If you want to read more, there's a very detailed article by Nicole Chabot mentioned in the resources at the end of this chapter.

 "I've never been consciously aware of a link between my sexuality and my body image, but having been asked the question, here's what occurred to me. If anything, being lesbian frees me up from some of the constraints and expectations that are put on women (and on men) to conform to certain ways of looking and acting. Our society is filled with images of how women should look - and much of the time, these images of women are framed in the context of 'this is how you should look if you want to get a man'.

"Because I'm not trying to get or please or appeal to men I think that, on some level, I have released myself from this pressure. Sure, some of it still gets to me (I am currently trying to lose half a stone - like most women I know!) But I don't feel quite the same weight of expectation around my body as I think some of my heterosexual women friends do. That's not to say I don't care how I look. It just - for me - takes away a bit of the pressure to conform to a particular image of how society says women should look."
Liz

But it's really important to remember that there is no single lesbian or gay body ideal, just as there isn't for heterosexual people. For example, amongst lesbian women there are the butch or feminine ways of looking and amongst gay men there are many different 'tribes', with the definitions involving physical appearance.

Sometimes these different appearances are not offered as ideals but codes of recognition, creating a strong bond within communities. This can mean an even greater desire to conform to your code and an even greater focus on appearance.

Some evidence suggests that lesbians tend to be able to build a more positive body image after they've come out while gay men more often find the opposite, perhaps because the various 'perfect' images of gay men are hard to achieve and may involve unhealthy eating patterns.

You'll notice this is a short chapter. That's because there's not a very strong or well-documented connection between body image and sexuality. Some gay people I spoke to said they couldn't think of any reason why body image would be different for them compared to heterosexual people. But for some – and seemingly more often for gay men – there is an extra set of pressures around appearance, so I didn't want to ignore those pressures.

BODY BOOST

Create a big poster for your room with an inspiring message on it. It could be 'Life gets better – I will make it happen' or 'I am not alone and nor are you' or 'Some people are gay – get over it'.

Summing up

In some ways, body image pressures are the same regardless of sexual orientation: anyone can have anxieties and dissatisfaction. But there can sometimes be extra pressures on people who are homosexual. These pressures may sometimes be greater while the individual is getting to grips with their sexuality and before they come out to the people around them.

After that, it seems that statistically gay men are likely (but not certain) to develop a more negative body image than lesbian women or heterosexual men and that they may feel a greater need to have a body that fits into a particular set of appearances. The pressures to have a particular body shape can be linked to low self-esteem and eating disorders.

If you're having trouble respecting and valuing your brilliant body, whether or not you think it's anything to do with how you feel about your sexuality, do seek help from one of the organisations at the end of this chapter.

RESOURCES FOR THIS CHAPTER

ONLINE

Young Stonewall – Stonewall is the UK's leading organisation supporting LGBTQ+ people, with the slogan 'Acceptance without exception'. Young Stonewall is their section for young people: www.youngstonewall.org.uk/

The It Gets Better Project: https://itgetsbetter.org/

The Trevor Project (US): www.thetrevorproject.org

Centre for Disease Control and Prevention – US site with resources on LGBT health here: www.cdc.gov/lgbthealth/youth-resources.htm

'How to Look the Part: 'Implications of Body Image Issues for Lesbian, Gay, and Bisexual College Students' by Nicole Chabot – a detailed academic article https://scholarworks.uvm.edu/cgi/viewcontent.cgi?referer=&httpsredir=1&article=1149&context=tvc

BOOKS

Fiction

The Shell House by Linda Newbery – a boy struggling with his homosexuality and religious intolerance and a story spanning 1917 and the present.

Boy Meets Boy by David Levithan – romantic comedy set in a high-school which sadly doesn't exist: one where everyone is free to be whoever they are and want to be.

Heartstopper by Alice Oseman – boy meets boy. A YA graphic novel in a school and sport setting.

Non-fiction

This Book is Gay by Juno Dawson – everything about coming out as gay.

BODY DYSMORPHIC DISORDER

WHAT IS BODY DYSMORPHIC DISORDER?

Body Dysmorphic Disorder (BDD and sometimes Body Dysmorphic Syndrome) is a type of mental health disorder and has connections with OCD (Obsessive Compulsive Disorder). The word comes from two ancient Greek words: *dys* meaning 'bad, wrong or negative' and *morphos* meaning 'shape', and this includes not only shape but other aspects of physical appearance. Dysmorphia means having a very disordered view of one's own shape, an extreme negative body image. People with BDD often also have anxiety disorders, eating disorders or depression.

> *"As a young teenager, I was convinced I was enormous. Looking back at photos of that time I didn't recognise myself as I was somewhere between normal and thin."*
> **Sheila**

You know that none of us perceives our own appearance accurately and many people are overly critical of their own appearance. But people with BDD have an extreme version of this and their worries about their body interfere with them living a healthy, active, normal life. They find themselves unable to stop thinking about the body parts they hate. These thoughts are intrusive and overwhelming.

Symptoms may not be the same from day to day. There will be better days and worse ones, often linked to other anxieties in one's life.

There are two main symptoms of BDD: obsessive feelings or thoughts and compulsive behaviours.

→ OBSESSIVE FEELINGS

People with BDD become obsessed with their hatred of their body or some aspect of it. They believe they're repulsive in some way – for example their weight or shape or face or skin – and that everyone must be noticing the feature that they hate and thinking how ugly they are. When someone tries to reassure them, they can't believe the reassurance.

"As a teenager I was obsessed that my nose was big. Also my hands. When I looked at my hands, they weren't, but when I didn't look at them I felt they were monster hands. With my nose, I also saw it as big in the mirror (though it probably felt bigger than it looked). I used to dream about having surgery to correct it. I didn't go to a doctor but I held out the promise to myself that one day I would. But somehow, at some point, I just stopped thinking about it. Now, I wouldn't say I have a small nose but I don't think about it. I know it's a normal nose – it's just mine not

anyone else's. Our perceptions and feelings change.
I wish I'd known."
Marie

The perceived flaws could be an exaggeration of something
that exists in a tiny way. Their nose might be slightly wider than
average; they might be taller or heavier than average; they might
have a small scar or blemish. In the mind of the BDD sufferer
these features become enormous and unavoidable.

Sometimes the flaws don't exist at all. BDD sufferers see
themselves as ugly or fat or believe that they have uneven skin or
repulsive hands or feet when there's nothing anyone else would
see at all.

The person thinks about these things obsessively. They may
have phases of doing this even more than usual, which can be
triggered by anxiety about something else. Or the phases could
be triggered by the knowledge of some public event coming up,
such as needing to perform in front of the class or go to a party.
The sufferer becomes fixated on the thought that everyone will
be looking at them and thinking how awful they look. This can
make them avoid public situations. It can also make them have
compulsive behaviours.

Cosmetic surgery

Sufferers may also become obsessed about the possibility of
having surgery or another procedure, which they believe will solve
their dysmorphia. Research[25] indicates that patients with severe
BDD who have a cosmetic treatment are usually not satisfied with
the result. The problem is that people with BDD have disordered
thinking: they believe their body is at fault, when it's actually
their mind. They think that changing their body will cure the

25 https://mghocd.org/desperately-seeking-surgery-the-truth-behind-body-
dysmorphic-disorder-and-plastic-surgery/

problem, but too often they are wrong, potentially leading to more dissatisfaction.

When people visit a cosmetic surgeon to ask about surgery, the surgeon should screen them for BDD, because of the high risk that surgery won't help them. But patients are often reluctant to discuss this with a surgeon and, unfortunately, too many surgeons don't automatically screen for BDD. Surgeons can't cure BDD so it is extremely important to consult someone who properly understands the implications of the condition rather than just offering surgery as a commercial transaction.

COMPULSIVE BEHAVIOURS

These could be things like:

🍀 **Looking in mirrors a lot or desperately avoiding mirrors**

🍀 **Refusing to have photos taken and becoming very anxious about them**

🍀 **Taking elaborate steps to hide the area – wearing thick make-up or a scarf to disguise it**

🍀 Picking skin to make it smoother

🍀 **Constantly asking people for reassurance – but not believing it**

🍀 **Constantly looking at models – as well as comparing oneself to other people**

🍀 Refusing to go out

🍀 **Examining every inch of skin in extreme detail, focusing on pores and tiny marks.**

Some of those are normal as occasional behaviours. For example, there's nothing wrong with choosing clothes or make-up that suits your shape or face and colouring; or checking your appearance before going out; or asking a friend if you look OK; and lots of people hate having photos taken. It's only a problem when those actions are very frequent and when they come from obsession and compulsion, rather than sensible, controlled decisions.

A diagnosis of BDD comes when a sufferer is severely distressed by symptoms and can't function properly at work or socially. Everyone is different and some will have milder symptoms than others but BDD is more than having the 'normal' range of negative body image that many people will be familiar with. BDD makes life really tough. Sufferers often don't want to leave the house and may not be able to face going to school or work or on holiday or family trips.

> *"My well-meaning parents put me on a diet aged seven, the start of years of diets and disordered eating. I was constantly told that I was fat because I was lazy and greedy. (I'm sure they didn't actually say this but it was the message I heard.) Even when not overweight, my mental image was a fat, ugly person. In my family, we did not express feelings well so food became how I coped with emotions, through periods of binge-eating, self-hatred and unsuccessful diets. It was many years before I could look at my body without disgust, helped by counselling and other women's writings on the subject."*
> **Rachael**

We don't know how common BDD is, partly because of different ways of measuring and partly because many people don't go to the doctor, as they may feel ashamed and may not think there's any treatment. (They shouldn't feel ashamed and there is treatment!) Various studies suggest anything between just under 1 per cent and almost 2.5 per cent of the general population of the US. It's more common than that in people with other mental illnesses such as depression.

People of all ages and genders can have BDD, but it's more common in teenagers and young adults, linked to the fact your bodies and minds are going through so much change.

BDD can be accompanied by depression – and even suicidal thoughts and, occasionally, actual suicide – so it's very important to go to a doctor for a diagnosis and help. But, even if you don't think you're depressed and you've never had suicidal thoughts, why spoil your life and your ability to succeed at school, work and socially, with unhelpful negative thoughts?

Self-harm can also be associated with BDD. If you are ever tempted or drawn towards self-harm, it's really important to get expert help.

BDD is not something to be ashamed of. As with other anxiety disorders, it's not your fault. It doesn't mean you are vain or narcissistic. It means that some of your thinking patterns are wrong, triggering unhelpful, unhealthy and extremely distressing and often disabling anxiety.

BODY BOOST

Be kind to your body: it deserves your gratitude and has done nothing wrong. So, indulge it: have a luxurious bath, massage oil into your feet; give yourself a manicure; exfoliate your face and use luxurious cream; put your hands on your shoulders or thighs and feel their strength and appreciate them for doing their best.

What causes BDD?

We simply don't know what tips someone from having a common level of negative body image into this distressing disorder. People with BDD often have other mental health disorders, too, and it can be difficult to untangle the causes. Traumatic early childhood experiences could play a part. There may be a genetic link. Or it may be an imbalance of brain chemicals with a cause that we don't know.

Muscle Dysmorphic Disorder

MDD is a specific type of BDD and involves the sufferer being obsessed with not being muscly enough. It is quite difficult to tell the difference between someone who is obsessed with working out and building muscle and someone who is doing so while wrongly believing they are not muscly. Someone with MDD genuinely believes their muscles are weak and small when they're actually within the normal range.

MDD is more common in men than women, because being muscly is a more common goal for men, though it's entirely possible for anyone to suffer it. The MDD sufferer will spend excessive time in the gym and be very distressed at missing a session; they will examine and think about muscle size even when not at the gym; they may restrict and control eating to the extent of an eating disorder; and generally their life is dominated by the compulsion to increase muscle size because of physical appearance rather than health and fitness.

MDD is sometimes referred to in the media as bigorexia, which is an inaccurate word. MDD is not an eating disorder, although it might lead to one.

> "My body seemed to grow in front of my eyes if I was uncomfortable or distressed. If a guy looked at me inappropriately, it felt like my body would grow until I filled the whole room. If I was going to a party I would obsess about what to wear, my body seeming to get bigger with every dress change and as my anxiety grew, until eventually I wouldn't go at all."
>
> **Luna, young adult**

→ Treatment for BDD

Treatment will depend on how severe your condition is, how long you've had it and what treatment is available where you live. There are three types of treatment:

1. **Talking therapy, usually Cognitive Behavioural Therapy (CBT).** This is a common treatment for mental health problems. It helps you see that your thinking is faulty and shows you how to change that thinking. A repeated thought is only a pathway in your brain, which grew because the thought kept being repeated, and the solution is to replace it with a correct and healthy thought. CBT can be one-to-one or in a group.

Part of the CBT will usually involve a particular therapy called 'exposure and response prevention' (ERP). You'll be gradually exposed to what's making you anxious and trained to respond healthily, so you feel less anxious and more in control. I'll talk a bit more about CBT on page 180.

2. **An anti-depressant called an SSRI.** There are various types and different ones will be appropriate for different people. It is essential only to take these under the guidance of a doctor as there can be serious side-effects, including suicidal thoughts, particularly for people under 30. It can take several weeks for them to work, so you'll need lots of support during this time. But when they work they can work very well.

3. CBT *and* an SSRI.

It's essential only to follow personal medical advice from someone who is not only an expert on your disorder, but also in treating people your age. Never take a medication prescribed for someone else as it may have very different and more dangerous effects for you. Anyone – particularly young people – taking anti-depressants and other drugs affecting the mind should be closely and regularly monitored by a doctor. Report any side-effects immediately, especially any change in your thoughts and especially any thoughts of suicide.

If these treatments don't work after some months, you can be referred for more specialist treatment. As with any mental illness, never give up if the first solutions you're offered don't work. Sometimes, you need more time, a different treatment or a different therapist. Sometimes, things in your life or other aspects of your mental state or development need to change, so a cure can take some time. But you do not have to feel like this forever: with all mental illnesses, there is hope of a positive outcome.

"I was very, very stubborn on my thoughts that I was fat, that my stomach was huge, that I was so ugly – nothing and no one could change my mind. I would get into fights with friends or therapists when they tried to change my mind because I was so insistent on my beliefs."
Freya

Summing up

Body Dysmorphic Disorder is a mental health disorder in which people strongly believe that there is something disgusting about their body. Their self-hatred is so strong that it affects many aspects of their life and can dominate their thoughts. It affects all genders and ages, but more often younger people than older. BDD responds to medical help, which is likely to be CBT talking therapy, or specific medication, or both. If you think you have BDD, please talk to a trusted adult or go to see a doctor. There is no need to be embarrassed or ashamed. Your mind just needs help getting back on track.

RESOURCES FOR THIS CHAPTER

ONLINE

NHS (UK): www.nhs.uk/conditions/body-dysmorphia/

The BDD Foundation: https://bddfoundation.org/

Mind: www.mind.org.uk/information-support/types-of-mental-health-problems/body-dysmorphic-disorder-bdd/#.W8TPChNKhMU

'Imperfect Me – the impact of body dysmorphia': www.youtube.com/watch?v=OVklwL5odLc

Distorted body images by Matthew R Longo: www.apa.org/science/about/psa/2013/12/body-representations.aspx

Mirror box therapy: www.physio-pedia.com/Mirror_Therapy

Problems of cosmetic surgery for those with BDD: www.ncbi.nlm.nih.gov/pmc/articles/PMC5986110/#bb0145

The 'Pathways' Powerpoint on my website: go to www.nicolamorgan.com and put 'pathways' in the search box. Or go to: www.slideshare.net/NicolaMorgan1961/stress-well-for-schools-31-pathways-exercise

BOOKS

Non-fiction

Body Image Problems and Body Dysmorphic Disorder by Lauren Callaghan, Annemarie O'Connor and Chloe Catchpole

chapter *eight*

LIVING WITH VISIBLE (OR INVISIBLE) DIFFERENCE

Lots of people have more obvious reasons than others for feeling noticeably different. Sometimes this is because they have something out of the ordinary about them that is visible to others – perhaps scarring, a facial deformity, or a missing or extra limb. Sometimes the difference isn't visible to most other people, but the person themselves knows about it and knows that it makes their body different from others – perhaps an illness that requires regular medical treatment, such as diabetes, or a condition that means their stomach or bowels don't work properly.

WHEN DIFFERENCES ARE DISFIGUREMENTS

You know everyone is different and there are loads of versions of 'normal'. I've discussed how the models we see most often represent only a small percentage of the body shapes out there.

And you know many people are quite negative about themselves, even when their features are within the usual range of how humans are: different, varied and individual. But there are times when something does happen and a person has a visible feature that makes them stand out in a way that might seem negative or challenging, at least at first.

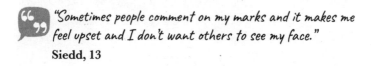

"Sometimes people comment on my marks and it makes me feel upset and I don't want others to see my face."
Siedd, 13

The organisation, Changing Faces, has excellent information to help raise awareness and understanding of all the aspects of living with visible differences. They use the word 'disfigurement' because it has a legal definition, although they acknowledge that some people don't like the word, preferring 'visible difference'. They also point out that usually we should use a phrase that describes what has happened to the person, such as saying they were born with a cleft lip, or that they were scarred in a fire.

Types of visible difference

There are so many ways that someone might look different. You might be born with a large birthmark on your face, gigantism or dwarfism, an assymetrical jaw or other facial features, or any one of many other conditions. A common condition is a cleft lip and/or palate, where a baby is born with a split in their lip and sometimes roof of their mouth; this can be treated by surgery soon after birth, but there is usually some scarring to the lip, though this can be almost unnoticeable. You might develop alopecia (baldness) or a cancer that requires surgery to remove part of your body and such things can happen at any stage of life. You could have a skin condition, perhaps severe eczema, or scarring from burns, or stretch marks or any other marks. Your visible difference could have a name, such as Crouzon's

Syndrome (which affects the growth of your cheekbones) or no name, or you might have scars from self-harm. If so, there's a resource at the end of this chapter for you.

There are millions of people in the world who have such challenges and who face unwanted attention, discrimination, intrusive questioning, low expectations at school or in work, and all manner of stereotyping in the media and from people they meet. There'll be several people in your school who are dealing with these experiences. And yet we are all exactly the same underneath: sometimes fragile, sometimes strong, always human.

People might not be deliberately cruel (though they often are), but even a look that lingers, or inquisitive comments or patronising remarks, mean that for the individual concerned it can be hard to be treated the same as everyone else. In other words, discrimination is likely.

Visible differences can happen to anyone, regardless of background, success, intelligence, money, personality. Even modern cosmetic surgery often can't remove all signs of the difference. And many people are happy with how they look anyway.

Dealing with visible difference

What does it do to someone's body image when they have something about them that visibly stands out? How would it make someone with a scar or twisted spine feel when villains in stories are often portrayed with scars or hunched backs? Would it make a difference if someone was born with their condition – such as the conjoined twins, Tippi and Grace, in Sarah Crossan's *One* or August, the facially deformed boy in RJ Palacio's *Wonder*? Or it might be something that happened to them later – such as Izzy in Cynthia Voigt's *Izzy, Willy Nilly*, who loses a leg in a car crash, or Deenie in Judy Blume's *Deenie*, about a girl who is quite nasty and cruel but then develops a curved spine (scoliosis) and has to rethink her attitudes to others, developing empathy through her own experience?

"I had terrible eczema as a child. It was open and sore and looked horrible. Kids at school called me 'Scabber' and wouldn't choose me for teams and refused to sit next to me in class. They'd say, 'Please Miss, I don't want to catch her infection.' The more I covered it up, the worse it got. One day I just thought 'to hell with it', and stopped covering it up. The less I worried and tried to hide it, the better it got. Eventually I grew out of it, just when the bullies all got teen acne!"

Dawn

The answer to those questions is that it depends on the individual. If someone has looked different from an early age, they might find they cared less about trivial things that other people bother about. Or they might be increasingly angry and want to lash out at people making careless comments or when they see themselves being treated negatively. Someone might end up campaigning for better recognition of their condition or promoting body positivity. They might find it really difficult or they might find it easier than you might imagine. Their friends and parents and teachers might be supportive and wise, or not. Their personalities could be a help or hindrance. Every life is different. No one should ever assume they know what someone else's life is like.

In those novels I mentioned, we see a whole variety of situations and personalities and lives. Deenie lacks support from her parents, who are bad role models in various ways. Izzy has friends who seem cool, but who don't cope or support her well. She makes a new and very uncool friend whose honesty and individuality help Izzy work through the huge change to her previously blessed life. Conjoined Grace and Tippi deal with their extraordinary situation from two separate personality styles and have to deal daily with intense curiosity and shock from people who see them – and it's those people who have the most to learn and change, rather than the two girls. And August, the boy with the face so deformed that he says he won't describe what he looks like because 'whatever you're thinking, it's probably worse', deals with people's reactions with enormous humour.

BODY BOOST

Draw a picture of yourself, focusing on all the great things your body can do. You can choose whether to highlight or hide your disfigurement: your body, your choice.

VISIBLE DIFFERENCE AND SOCIAL MEDIA

There are two sides to this. On the positive side, people can easily communicate with others with similar experiences on social media, getting support and sharing stories and advice. It becomes easier for someone with a rare condition not to feel alone and for someone who doesn't want to go out much (or at all) still to have friends and support. And you might find it more relaxing to have fun online and unseen sometimes (though you shouldn't feel you have to).

The negatives come from the appalling cruelty that some people show online. These cruel, ignorant people are a minority, but even one grotesque personal insult is too many. There are stories of people receiving appalling comments after they've been on television or their picture has been shared online. The Changing Faces report contains some of these incidents. One that stood out for me was a woman who said that after she had appeared on TV to talk about her condition, she received a message from another woman saying that people like her shouldn't be allowed on television. By any standards, that is disgusting, inhuman and beyond ignorant.

BODY BOOST

Express yourself in writing. You don't have to write about yourself (though you can) but make up a story that reflects your feelings or a point you'd like to make. Or you could write to a local newspaper or magazine with your experience. (Be careful: they will want a photo and you might find it intrusive, so discuss with your adults first.)

We all need *to call out* such behaviour whenever we see it. The social media companies also have a role here and they often do not do nearly enough to make sure that such shocking behaviour is punished or prevented. There should be zero tolerance. Otherwise, what kind of human are we?

Reflecting the real world

We also need to see many more examples of visible difference on our screens and in all types of media, not to showcase them but because that would reflect how the real world is. As one respondent to a major report for Changing Faces said, 'Disfigurement just doesn't exist in the media. We're invisible, and that says to me that the people running media companies don't care about us. Yes, you see more people in wheelchairs in programmes, but where are people who look different? Where are the birthmarks? Where are the burn scars? It's pathetic.'

Jen Campbell, an author who also has a genetic condition called EED, which involves various visible differences including to fingers, teeth and hair, has spoken eloquently about this lack of representation and also how people with visible difference are so often portrayed as the villains in stories. You'll find references in the resources at the end of the chapter.

"I was born with EEC Syndrome (Ectrodactyly Ectodermal Dysplasia Clefting Syndrome). This means that I was born with more or less of certain things. I have missing fingers and misshapen teeth. It also affects my hair (alopecia), eyes, skin and kidneys. I spent a lot of time in hospital as a child as doctors reshaped my fingers to help me function as best I could. Growing up, other children tended to be very open about discussing my condition and accepting of it. It was adults who were wary. I think this has a lot to do with trying to be polite but, if we don't discuss these topics, ignorance occurs. I think it also has to do with media representation of disfigurement and disability. All too often in films the 'bad guy' is someone with scars or differently abled; disfigurement, historically and even today, is used as a marker for evil. Think of James Bond villains, Roald Dahl's The Witches, Disney's Scar, Captain Hook... the list is endless.

"Disfigurement and disability also often appear in over-sentimental inspiration stories. These films/books are mostly made by able-bodied people and the end result is a product that seeks to make the able-bodied viewer or reader feel good because they have empathised with someone different. Whilst empathy is to be encouraged, if these stories don't include good research and representation, this causes problems. Overall, the narratives surrounding disability and disfigurement in mainstream media need

more nuance. We need creatives from within the disability community and those with disfigurements to be involved so we can further a constructive and diverse conversation."
Jen Campbell

But the internet and social media also provide lots of help and information. There are new support groups all the time so do keep up-to-date with what's out there. Most people are basically decent: we just need to be educated sometimes.

INVISIBLE DIFFERENCES

There are many conditions which mean that someone's body works in a different way. If you have one of these conditions, you are probably already very well-informed and I hope you have good support from doctors and other therapists. You've probably already been online and found organisations to support you with the best advice. Those organisations usually also offer ways for you to communicate with other people with your condition. They can give you the best advice, of course.

 "Invisible disabilities affect body image. My 14-year-old daughter was diagnosed with type 1 diabetes aged 10, so has to inject insulin. For a long time, she refused to use a pump. She said that wearing a device permanently attached to her would make her feel different. Eventually she saw the benefit, and now brazens it out incredibly well, but her attitude may change as she gets older. I know of many teenagers who've abandoned their devices or neglect their diabetes, risking their lives, because they feel self-conscious injecting."
Helen

You may – or may not – find that your condition affects your body image in several ways. You may feel that your body is 'imperfect'. But remember: there's no such thing as perfection! You may find that your condition means you can't stop thinking about your body and feeling that other people are looking at you differently, negatively or even pityingly – if they are, it's their problem. You may be angry about what's happened to you. If those negative emotions dominate your life, ask about some counselling to help you realise that all bodies are different and that, whatever the challenges you face, you can face them and they do not need to define you or spoil your ability to achieve great things.

All those feelings – and many more – are entirely understandable. You may also go through phases of particularly strong feelings. You may even reject the treatment you need to take, trying to believe, for example, that the doctors must be wrong and that they can't possibly know how you feel. Again, this is a really understandable reaction. I think the best way to deal with it is to be as well-informed as possible about your condition and the options, and to make contact with as many other people as possible who have dealt with what you're going through.

You are not alone. And you do have a ***brilliant body***, not because of what it can't do but because of what it can do.

BODY IMAGE AND BLINDNESS ←

When I started writing this book and thinking about how our mental picture of ourselves is built, I wondered: 'How do you know what you look like when you can't see what you look like? What kind of mental picture of yourself – body image – might you have?' I also wondered whether blind people would care more or less, or just the same, about their appearance. So, as with all the other topics, I did research and talked to people with the experience.

Of course, many people who are registered blind do have some sight and many have had more sight in the past. And those who are partially sighted have devices, such as lighted magnifying mirrors to help them see details of their face a bit better, as well as the opportunity to use smartphone cameras to gain a closer idea of what they look like. (Though, as I said in chapter one, photos give us a particular and often different image to reality.)

> "I never saw what I looked like till at 22 a friend took a close-up photo and I looked with an electronic magnifier, in black and white. Things have changed now: people can take photos on a phone and check make-up. I decided amazing make-up would be easier than normal make-up so I used eye shadow and liner to make clouds. I wore different colour nail varnishes. I found that being eccentric along with mad make-up hid any problems with my outfits."
>
> **Tess**

Remember that sight is not the only way we build a mental picture of ourselves: we also feel and touch our bodies, which gives us a sense of our shape and features. We have proprioception – that sense of our body and the space it's taking up. And we have the information that comes from other people's comments. Partially or unsighted people have to rely on those sources of information more than others – and remember that they are not accurate. Everyone's body image is built up from a mass of complex information that we've been receiving all our lives and only a part of that comes from sight. It may be the most obvious part to people who are sighted, but it's very far from the whole story.

Research doesn't show us whether blind people have a more inaccurate body image than others, but it makes sense that they would, simply because sight is the most accurate (though not perfect) sense providing information about appearance. There is some research[26] that suggests that young people with visual impairment are somewhat more likely to feel negative about their bodies. But other research suggests that people (females, in this small study[27]) born blind may have more positive body image than those who become blind later and also than sighted women. These studies are small, so don't take them as proof.

Feeling self-conscious

One thing we do know from research based on interviews and experiences is that blind people care about their appearance as much as anyone else does. Some more than others, just as amongst sighted people and any other group. It makes sense that blind people could be self-conscious, because if you don't know exactly what you look like it would be easy to worry a lot about it. And self-consciousness was a word that kept coming up during my own conversations and research. A blind person, not being able to see themselves in detail, often feels very watched by other people.

 "I went to special school for the blind and partially sighted. This sheltered experience may have protected my self-image, as I wasn't exposed to fashion and models. But we were all very conscious who had their first bra and what size! Being too fat or thin never entered my head: I ate what I liked and so did my friends. I remember

26 Pinquart and Pfeiffer 2012 https://journals.sagepub.com/doi/abs/10.1177/0264619612458098

27 Baker, Sivyer, Towell 1998 https://onlinelibrary.wiley.com/doi/abs/10.1002/%28SICI%291098-108X%28199811%2924%3A3%3C319%3A%3AAID-EAT10%3E3.0.CO%3B2-R

being desperate for shoes that had a heel so they would echo down the corridor but when I got them I didn't like everyone hearing me walk..."
Tess

Practical problems arise, such as difficulty in applying make-up, or not knowing whether colours 'go'. Some people decide to use this as an opportunity to look deliberately different, expressing themselves in very bright clothes or very distinctive make-up or hair styles.

Exercise

The issue of weight can be important because a blind person is as likely as anyone else to be satisfied or dissatisfied with weight and shape but it's often not so easy to exercise as it is for an able-bodied, sighted person. Walking fast is a challenge, for example, and all sorts of exercise activities are more difficult to engage with.

As with anything that makes one person's life more challenging than another, there will be fantastic advice and support from the various organisations that support your situation. Through them, and if necessary with help from the medical profession, you'll be able to connect with other people just like you, and sharing experiences and advice is an excellent way to get to know how to respect and celebrate your brilliant body and to use it well.

BODY BOOST

With a friend or adult, work out a quick, simple, strong explanation for whatever it is that people want to ask about. Practise saying it. Once you've said it, people will usually stop wondering about it.

WHAT CAN YOU DO TO UNDERSTAND MORE?

Whether you have a visible difference yourself or whether you know someone who does and you want a better understanding, there's lots of expert advice and experienced support. You'll find that online (both in official organisations and self-help groups), through your own doctors, and from your local library.

Changing Faces has some really practical advice, including how to help you (or your friend) deal with other people's reactions as well as your own feelings.

> "Two years ago, one of my closest friends had a brain bleed. She has gone through such an incredible journey from learning how to walk, talk and eat all over again and she continues to impress me every day. However, she began to think she didn't fit and she wanted to change her appearance and behaviour, Unfortunately, she is now diagnosed with depression and anorexia. She communicated her feelings to me and I had to make her aware of the help she could get and she is now having close medical attention. I know she was perfect already and she didn't need to change and I think she knows that now."
> **Jess, 16**

I think it's really important for everyone who doesn't have a visible difference to read as much as possible about these topics. Reading other people's stories and viewpoints builds our empathy and gives us the tools we all need to create a decent, active community of human beings with all our countless differences.

Summing up

A significant number of people live with visible and invisible differences which can affect their self-image as well as the way other people treat them. There is an enormous variety of such differences and ways in which people are affected. But there's lots of help, too, whether medical or surgical opportunities or organisations providing information or groups offering support.

We should also remember that many people have no wish to change their visible difference and can have really positive body image. And let's hold onto the fact that most people aren't cruel: they may be ignorant or inexperienced and not know what to say or not say but the more you share your feelings, the more quickly people will learn how to behave fairly and decently to each other.

RESOURCES FOR THIS CHAPTER

ONLINE

Changing Faces UK offers help for every type of visible difference: www.changingfaces.org.uk

Survey 2017 report: www.changingfaces.org.uk/wp-content/uploads/2017/05/DITUK.pdf

Vlogger Nikki Lilly, who has a visible difference, talks about make-up and baking: www.youtube.com/channel/UC4RH7UBW2_c8qUP2qcF6zmQ

Coping with self-harm scars: www.inourhands.com/wp-content/uploads/2015/03/ self-harm-advice-for-exposing-your-scars1.pdf

Katie Piper is a model who was severely disfigured after an acid attack. She is now a body confidence campaigner: www.katiepiperfoundation.org.uk

Author, Jen Campbell, discusses visible difference on her YouTube channel: https://bit.ly/2zil2mL under the heading 'Videos about disfigurement/representation'.

She has several videos about the importance of seeing yourself in the media and about the portrayal of villains and deformity, for example. Very articulate and powerful.

Blogging Astrid, on blindness: https://bloggingastrid.com/2016/02/12/when-i-look-in-the-mirror-blindness-and-body-image/

BOOKS

Fiction

Wonder by RJ Palacio – August was born with an extremely disfigured face. His weapon is humour, but the people at his new school have a lot to learn.

Izzy, Willy Nilly by Cynthia Voigt – Izzy loses her leg. She loses her image of perfection, too, including in the eyes of her shallow friends. But she makes a new, surprising friend.

One by Sarah Crossan – extraordinary story of conjoined 16-year-old twins, Grace and Tippi.

Tall Story by Candy Gourlay – Andi's half-brother, Barnardo, is eight foot tall. Seen through Andi's eyes.

Deenie by Judy Blume – her mother dreams of a modelling career for her but Deenie develops scoliosis (curvature of the spine). Both must overcome their prejudices and change mindset. Only one will succeed.

Faceless by Alyssa Sheinmel – a girl has a face transplant after her face is destroyed by lightning.

Firegirl by Tony Abbott – (not recommended if you have major facial scarring but recommended for your peers) – through the eyes of a boy who experiences the brief stay at his school of a girl with severe scars.

Out of my Mind by Sharon M Draper – Melody has cerebral palsy and is very bright, but people don't see past her communication difficulties. Gripping and searing.

chapter nine
EATING DISORDERS AND SELF-HARM

Some of the most distressing problems associated with negative body image are eating disorders and self-harm. It's also important to add that even discussing these can be triggering for sufferers with such disorders. So, if that's you, please make sure you talk to an adult who understands your condition if anything you read in this chapter makes you feel distressed.

 "Anyone with an eating disorder feels very isolated, is super sensitive and self-punishing. They need compassion and understanding, and for people to see that they're in pain, without them needing to prove it with the typical behaviours of an eating disorder."

Rose, young adult

WHAT ARE EATING DISORDERS?

Eating disorders are serious mental and physical illnesses that make it almost impossible to eat and exercise normally. They come with high levels of distress, heightened risk of suicide and serious – sometimes fatal – physical effects. In spite of popular belief, sufferers are not in control of their eating and it's not just 'a phase'. They need expert help for their mind and behaviours to return to normal. With early, specialised treatment, young people can have complete recovery.

BODY BOOST

Start looking at photos online of 'body positive' people and see how confident they are in their bodies. Looking at pictures of glamorous curvy people can start to change how you think about fat.

Eating disorders usually – but not always – come with a fear of being fat and with a distorted body image. They all involve some degree of restricted, irregular eating, which affect the brain's functioning with regard to appetite, mood, thinking and compulsions. The most common trigger is an illness or diet that leads to weight loss in an individual who also has other risk factors. Indeed, eating disorders are believed to arise from a complex mix of genetics, personality, psychological and environmental factors. They affect all genders, ages and ethnic groups.

Types of eating disorder

The best-known eating disorders are anorexia nervosa, bulimia nervosa and binge-eating disorder. With binge-eating disorder, sufferers have repeated out-of-control episodes of eating large quantities. Their eating can be restrictive at other times, as they try to regain control. Binge episodes are also typical of bulimia, except that people with bulimia also have an overwhelming compulsion to purge (make themselves vomit or use laxatives). Anorexia literally means 'without appetite' but this does not properly describe the symptoms. Sufferers have little choice but to restrict food to an unhealthy or dangerous level, usually accompanied by a compulsion to over-exercise. Some can only eat tiny amounts, while others (with the binge-purge type of anorexia) have moments of eating well, followed by purging.

"My most vivid memory is of sitting in PE, aged about 9, pinching my thighs and trying to pull out the tiny hairs on my legs. I thought everyone was staring and that my classmates wouldn't want to sit next to me because my body was disgusting.

"Each class would be weighed in public and it became a competition about being the smallest and lightest: that person got a lot of attention. I didn't understand why my body was getting heavier (though I was never overweight and was quite small for my age). I never knew that my body would change or grow and no one talked about it. I got more and more panicked about these weigh-ins and felt out of control, exposed and that my friendships were in jeopardy."

Luna, young adult

All these disorders are very dangerous and can be life-threatening. The longer they go on, the longer treatment might take. Treatment must be under expert supervision.

There are other eating disorders, too, all involving various forms of controlled eating in order to create a particular effect. Orthorexia, for example, is a condition where people are obsessed by what they believe is super-healthy eating. They can become severely malnourished.

It's not healthy to be obsessed by any type of eating. A true healthy diet is varied and enjoyable and has enough calories and nutrients to feed all parts of our bodies.

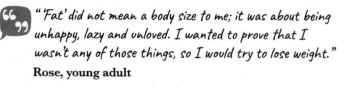

> "My own experience, from the many parents I talk with and my own daughter (and clinicians also comment on this anecdotally) is that health promotion initiatives and 'sizeist' bullying are the two most common triggers for an eating disorder. The mechanism is probably that after one of these two things, people restrict their food, and if they have a genetic vulnerability to an eating disorder, the weight loss kicks off the illness."
>
> **Eva Musby, Anorexiafamily.com**

→ WHAT ABOUT 'DISORDERED EATING'?

Many people don't have a specific named eating disorder but do have 'disordered eating', which means that they share some of the symptoms and behaviours of actual disorders around food and exercise. Each eating disorder has a particular list of symptoms and some people don't fall neatly into one set of symptoms. Disordered eating can sometimes become a disorder or it might just continue as a negative relationship with food, such as frequent dieting or patterns of restricting certain foods or having restrictive rules or rituals.

> "'Fat' did not mean a body size to me; it was about being unhappy, lazy and unloved. I wanted to prove that I wasn't any of those things, so I would try to lose weight."
>
> **Rose, young adult**

Some people with disordered eating will need expert help to regain a healthy eating pattern, while others will respond to good advice for self-help. People with eating disorders need expert help, beyond what any self-help advice can give.

WHAT'S THE CONNECTION WITH BODY IMAGE?

Eating disorders and negative body image are extremely closely linked. Not everyone who has eating disorders develops them because of negative body image but negative body image is usually a major part of the problem for a sufferer. People who have a very negative body image may try to change their shape by eating too little or exercising too much. Sometimes they think this gives them control over their body but then, of course, the eating disorder controls them: that's why it's a disorder or illness.

"My daughter (now 18) went through a phase of needing full make-up on a daily basis. She dyed her hair, and cared deeply how she was perceived. She became very ill with anorexia for a couple of years and was hospitalised. Since recovery she has a different outlook. She eats what she wants, and exercises. She wears make-up because she likes it, but not every day. She doesn't take notice of the opinions of others, and has taken up kickboxing. She's great!"
Lalla

Some sports have a higher risk of eating disorders because they focus more on weight and appearance than others. They may lead young people to interfere with normal eating – the most common trigger in those vulnerable to an eating disorder. There are sports where weight affects which group you're in, such as wrestling, horse-racing or rowing; or where a particular weight or body shape makes the sport easier, such as running, weight-lifting, cycling or swimming; or where appearance is a part of the whole picture, such as dancing, gymnastics, body-building, diving.

Since controlling food and exercise are such an obvious way in which we change aspects of our shape without involving cosmetic surgery, it's easy to see why many people try to do this and why some find themselves controlled by the illnesses of eating disorders.

Lots of people worry about becoming fat, but this doesn't necessarily lead to a disorder. Many teenage girls and boys use unhealthy weight control behaviours, such as skipping meals, counting calories or going for a run just to burn calories. Doing those things every now and then doesn't mean you have an eating disorder. Eating disorders involve compulsive behaviours: habits you can't stop and which become worse. Most young people who occasionally skip a meal will not develop an eating disorder.

"My 8-year-old daughter began having body issues after over-reacting to healthy-eating education classes and experiencing bullying at primary school. She had always been perceptive about images, both in real-life and in the media, but had not taken it personally until endlessly criticised by boys in the playground. 'Fat' was their favourite insult and high-achieving girls their target. Unfortunately, she found the insult difficult to shrug off and, although she was slim, she thought she was fat. Consequently, she tried to avoid school, was unhappy and *often refused to eat a range of treats. In the end we moved to a whole different environment, slower-paced, away from the pressures of metropolitan life and into an active outdoor lifestyle. Without excessive fashion and technology pressures, both my daughters are much more fulfilled and moving forward healthily, though competition still features."*

Claire

If you notice you have difficulties with regular eating and have anxious thoughts around food and weight, you should get help. You may not tick all the boxes for anorexia, bulimia or binge-eating disorder, yet still have a diagnosable eating disorder which is just as distressing and dangerous. For instance, some people have a form of anorexia without actually looking thin. You may be in the early stages of any of the eating disorders, which means that if you wait, you are likely to get worse. Experts recommend early intervention, so if you're in doubt, ask for help. Get this help from a doctor or from one of the mainstream organisations, not from other sufferers. Each person is different and you need reliable medical advice.

THE PROBLEM WITH TODAY'S MEDIA, ESPECIALLY ONLINE

Many studies have found links between seeing thin images in the media, desiring to be thin and developing disordered eating. And you've already seen how 'thin ideal' images dominate the media for women and how muscled, ripped ideals dominate for men. As I said, eating disorders arise from a mix of factors, but there's good reason to believe that the Internet and social media are part of the increasing problem, at least of disordered eating, although the picture is less clear for specific disorders.

"I developed anorexia at the end of my first year at art school. I only just managed to stay out of hospital but never had any real help. I found my body incredibly hard to accept: I am very tall, and I was horrified at outgrowing my sisters, my mother and my friends. It didn't feel feminine to be that size; it felt incredibly undesirable. It felt like the only way to cope with being so tall was to be very thin. Also, my exterior didn't seem to fit my interior. I felt very small, fragile, young, inadequate. Yet I was strapping and strong-featured. I was unable to accept this, and unable to live comfortably with it for a long time."

Frances

HOW ONLINE ACTIVITY MIGHT INCREASE DISORDERED EATING

There are so many adverts or plugs for losing weight, often wrapped up in what looks like science. You've probably seen adverts yourself for slimming products and regimes (especially if you're female) or muscle-building products and regimes (especially if you're male). It's hard to avoid the diets, fads and endorsements.

Technology makes it easy to manipulate images so that models look even thinner or more muscled than they are.

Social media makes it easy for diet fads to go viral and there are competitive 'games' aimed at young people. It can be hard to walk away from those trends if your friends are following them.

Body-shaming and fat-shaming happen so easily on social media. There were nasty comments about body shape before, of course, but it's easier for spiteful, thoughtless or bullying people to make such comments, because they don't have to see the reaction. Not seeing the reaction means that people who would not normally be bullies can fall into the trap of throwing insults around on social media. There's even a phrase for this: the 'online disinhibition effect' describes the finding that all sorts of people of different ages tend to be less careful and caring online. Absence of body language, facial expression and immediacy makes it easier to be cruel, either accidentally or deliberately.

The internet has a dangerous world of sites which pretend to support people with anorexia or bulimia but in fact help sufferers to become even more ill. Most sow the idea that these are healthy lifestyle choices. They're not: they're dangerous illnesses! If you have any kind of controlling relationship with food or desire to be thin, these sites are likely to be very triggering. Therefore, if you want facts and good advice, only go to websites which do not talk about eating disorders as a lifestyle. They are illnesses, with treatments.

> "Creating rituals around loving my body has helped a lot. Things like moisturising and placing my hands on my stomach and breathing. Or looking at my feet and thinking that they have never done anything to hurt me: they have carried me around this world and they deserve love and gratitude, not hatred and punishment."
>
> **Freya, young adult**

The internet can help. It's a matter of finding the right help: proper, informed support that will show you how to regain control of your mind. This involves respecting your body for all it can do, rather than trying to alter what it looks like.

What about self-harm?

Self-harm and eating disorders are two different sets of conditions but I have chosen to talk about them in the same chapter because they have some connections.

One

Some people with eating disorders also self-harm and when they do, the underlying causes are likely to be the same.

Two

Both have complex causes and many variations, but very negative body image can be (but is not always) a feature in both.

Three

Both involve negative coping actions for a usually hidden problem and those actions become repeated habits. As with all habits, they can be hard to stop and require expert help to do so.

Four

Many triggers and reasons why someone self-harms are similar to the triggers and reasons for an eating disorder.

Five

In both cases, some sufferers get pleasure from their actions and this makes them keep doing it.

Six

Both involve the individual continuing to inflict harm on themselves. So, in a way, both are self-harming.

~~~~~~

Self-harm comes in different forms, including cutting, burning, hair-pulling and repeated hitting. People describe various reasons why they are compelled to do this. There is almost always an underlying – and often deeply hidden – mental pain. Some people say the physical pain is preferable to mental pain. Some people say they hate their body and want to punish it. Some say they do it because they feel ashamed and worthless and not deserving of love and respect. Some people will know how or when their illness started, while others will not be able to identify the starting point.

 "Talking, sharing, being open and vulnerable with someone you feel safe with is the most healing thing and you will always feel better afterwards, even if it feels very scary at the time."

Freya, young adult

Research doesn't prove whether negative body image causes self-harm, but people who self-harm do often have negative body image. When they do, however, the harm isn't necessarily focused on the hated body area. It's more indirect than that: more a general self-hatred or a need to escape distress.

Luna, young adult

Obviously, self-harming can have lifelong physical effects in terms of scarring and it can be very dangerous. It also needs expert help and the earlier the better. You'll need good support from family, friends and school, but it's really important that this is properly informed support, as it's very easy for well-meaning people to say the wrong thing.

BODY BOOST

Make sure your family, friends and teachers know what to say and what not to say. People usually don't know how their comments might make things worse. Direct them to good websites, such as the ones at the end of this chapter.

One other thing that self-harm and eating disorders share: someone telling you that you have a beautiful body won't be enough to stop you continuing with the habit of hurting it. It's much deeper-rooted than that. Whether you're hurting your body by direct damage or starving it, you've formed a strong 'habit-loop' in your brain and it will take more than some well-meaning comments from people who love you to change that habit.

You are worth a lot. Your body is brilliant. But you'll need more than me or anyone else telling you so. I hope one day you will properly believe it. Because it's true.

"I used to think my body hated me, wanted me to be fat, hairy and spotty; but it wants me to be happy and healthy just like everyone's does. I learnt to listen to my body, to hear her need for nourishment. Your body has unconditional love for you — no matter how many times you pick a scab, your body will always try to patch the cut back up."

Rose, young adult

BODY BOOST

Find a creative passion: crafts, or woodwork, knitting, cooking? I recently went to the craft section of a big store and couldn't believe the opportunities! Something that can occupy your mind and stop you focusing on your body could be real therapy.

Summing up

Eating disorders and self-harm involve complicated illnesses that display themselves differently in different sufferers. Negative body image is often strongly associated with these disorders, even though it is not thought to be a cause.

When someone hates how their body is or compares themselves negatively to images around them, they might use food and exercise to change how they look. This can lead to disordered eating, where someone has an unhealthy relationship with food and may often restrict food or over-exercise. Some of those people will develop specific eating disorders.

Self-harm is another way that people react to hatred of their body or of something in their lives.

Eating disorders are serious and dangerous illnesses that need proper medical treatment and good support. People with disordered eating also need good advice and support so that they can switch their mindset to one which will allow them to lead a genuinely healthier life.

Your brilliant body needs food, respect and a positive lifestyle.

RESOURCES FOR THIS CHAPTER

Caution: even some of the best health websites or articles may contain adverts that focus on body shape in an unhealthy way. Never click on diet adverts. They only want to sell you something.

ONLINE

National Health Service (UK):
www.nhs.uk/conditions/eating-disorders/

Teen Mental Health: http://teenmentalhealth.org/understanding-self-injury-self-harm/

The NHS has an app called 'Calm Harm' that is especially for dealing with overwhelming feelings of hatred or emotional pain that can lead to a desire to self-harm.

Eva Musby – Eva is the mother of an anorexia sufferer and now a leading expert. Her website is for parents but clinicians and schools will find very up-to-date advice: https://anorexiafamily.com/ Here she shows what schools can (and shouldn't) do: https://anorexiafamily.com/health-promotion-ED-prevention-body-obesity-school

Dove Self-Esteem Project: www.dove.com/uk/dove-self-esteem-project/school-workshops-on-body-image-confident-me.html

Planet Health has great ways to learn about healthy eating: www.planet-health.org/

Body Image Health: http://bodyimagehealth.org/healthy-bodies-curriculum/

Aimed at men: www.psycom.net/eating-disorders-men and www.eatingdisorderhope.com/blog/appreciating-the-functionality-of-the-body-in-male-body-image

Aimed at LGBTQ+:
www.nationaleatingdisorders.org/learn/general-information/lgbtq

And Teen Vogue:
www.teenvogue.com/story/transgender-youth-eating-disorders

Why some sites are so dangerous:
www.healthline.com/health/why-pro-ana-sites-are-so-dangerous

Feast or Famine: 'Food and Children's Literature' by Fiona Dunbar:
www.cambridgescholars.com/feast-or-famine-food-and-childrens-
literature

National Eating Disorders Collaboration (Australia):
www.nedc.com.au
If you're worried about someone: www.nedc.com.au/support-and-
services/supporting-someone/what-to-say-and-do/

BOOKS

Fiction

If you have an eating disorder, some books *could* trigger your illness.
Check with an adult who knows you well before you read these.
If reading them makes you worried about anything, talk to a
trusted adult.

Jelly by Jo Cotterill – Jelly has always used humour to deflect teasing.
Trouble is, this means people think she doesn't care. And she does.

Summer's Dream by Cathy Cassidy – Summer will have to work *very*
hard to get into ballet school. And lose weight – dangerously. Great
insight into one way an eating disorder can start.

Jemima Small Versus the Universe by Tamsin Winter – Relentlessly
bullied for her weight, Jemima has to show the universe that she's
worth more than anyone. Brilliant book with a very clear anti-dieting
and anti-weight-loss message.

Non fiction/memoir

Misfit – one size does not fit all by Charli Howard – how modelling
for agencies demanding an impossibly thin shape contributed to her
eating disorders (and how she recovered).

chapter *ten*

HOW TO IMPROVE YOUR BODY IMAGE

You've heard lots of reasons why people have a negative body image and some of the unhappy links with that. And along the way, I hope you've taken on board some more positive ways of thinking. Before I come to how you can look after your body in lots of physical, practical, healthy ways, let's have one more look at our minds and how to help them behave more positively and respectfully towards our brilliant bodies.

If you suffer from eating disorders or body dysmorphic disorder; or if you self-harm; or maybe you're questioning your gender; or have a mental illness making your life difficult or miserable, you need to find expert help, usually starting with your own doctor. But if you just want to improve your body image, there are lots of useful self-help techniques that are definitely worth trying.

In fact, what I'm going to suggest is useful for all sorts of situations you'll meet in your life. It's based on Cognitive Behavioural Therapy or CBT, which is a common therapy for conditions where our thinking has become damagingly negative.

Cognitive Behavioural Therapy

In CBT, the therapist breaks down the problem into five aspects:

1. Situations: what is the problem situation(s)? When does it happen? For example, the problem might be that you fear getting undressed for PE at school.

2. Thoughts: what do you think when this happens? For example, do you think everyone is believing you're overweight or ugly?

3. Emotions: what are your emotions during it? For example, ashamed or worthless.

4. Physical feelings: what physical symptoms do you notice? For example, you might sweat, blush or feel dizzy.

5. Actions: what actions do you take? For example, you might avoid it by making yourself late for PE.

Understanding what you feel and what's going on in your head and body are a really important start. A therapist can then encourage you to look into some of the answers a bit more and challenge the thinking. But you can look at this yourself, too.

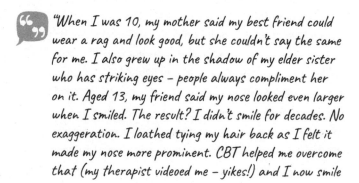

"When I was 10, my mother said my best friend could wear a rag and look good, but she couldn't say the same for me. I also grew up in the shadow of my elder sister who has striking eyes – people always compliment her on it. Aged 13, my friend said my nose looked even larger when I smiled. The result? I didn't smile for decades. No exaggeration. I loathed tying my hair back as I felt it made my nose more prominent. CBT helped me overcome that (my therapist videoed me – yikes!) and I now smile *a lot, even with my hair up! I wish I'd sought therapy earlier, but when I was at school there was no pastoral department. My message to young people is to talk about your feelings and use the support available: you are so lucky to have it."*

Shaheen

For example, believing that everyone is looking at you and thinking you're overweight and ugly can be challenged in several ways. If they're looking at you, how are they getting changed themselves? Do you think they think you're the most important thing to look at? Everyone has to be looking at something and how can they talk to you without looking at you? Might they also be self-conscious? What is the evidence that they think you're fat and ugly? They said so? Does that make it true – isn't it more likely to be just an ignorant insult? Is it their business? If they're looking at you, how rude and childish!

You see how it goes? These conversations challenge your emotions of shame, self-consciousness and worthlessness by changing your thinking.

BODY BOOST

Remember: a negative thought is just a pathway in your brain that you created and that you can change by replacing it with a different, more positive thought. Look at the 'Pathways' Powerpoint at the end of this chapter.

CBT is also different from some other therapies because it focuses directly on the problems you have now, rather than trying to find causes in your past. It's practical, looking for solutions. You'll probably be given 'homework', things to practise. You might be asked to write a diary. All this helps you recognise when thought patterns become unhelpful and to challenge them with new thinking.

WHAT CAN YOU DO YOURSELF?

Two things to adjust your negative thinking:

1. **Notice and challenge your negative or distressing thoughts.** Create a conversation in your head in which you question the thoughts. Why did you think that? What evidence do you have? Is that a helpful thought? Why are you hurting yourself? What would be a more useful thought?

2. **Notice when you're about to do something that will make you feel bad and instead do something else.** You're about to go online to look at images of beauty... go outside and watch the sunset instead. You're about to make yourself late for PE because you hate getting changed in public... take some deep breaths, put a smile on your face and repeat inside your mind: 'I can do this and it will benefit me'.

There are also various apps you can get, some of them free. And look for something called 'Guided self-help' where you don't have full-scale CBT, but you work through a self-help book with the guidance of a trained person.

THE PATHWAYS EXERCISE

Let me share my own version of CBT. It's called The Pathways
Exercise. It's based on how our brains have thoughts and beliefs.

Any thought – anything you believe, know or think – exists
because you created a pathway of neurons in your brain. This
applies whether it's a true fact (such as, that the capital of Spain
is Madrid or 10 x 10 = 100) or an opinion or belief (such as,
'I'm not popular' or 'I'm ugly'). If the thought is new or flimsy
– something you've only just learnt or you're not sure of – the
neural networks will be few and weak, so the thought can easily
be lost, forgotten or changed. For example, when you've only
just learnt that the capital of Mongolia is Ulaanbaatar, it's easy
to forget that fact. If you practise saying it, you'll be less likely
to forget it because you've created more and stronger pathways
in your brain. And if you also write it down, you'll create better
pathways and be even less likely to forget.

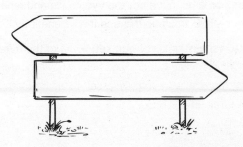

The more times you have a thought and the more it fits with what you already know, the stronger the pathways become and the harder it is to think differently. That's great when the thought is a true and useful fact, but not when it's false or negative.

So, if you thought the capital of Mongolia was Madrid, because someone had taught you that and you'd believed it and learnt it, it would be harder to learn and remember that in fact it is Ulaanbaatar.

And if the thought was that you are unpopular or ugly, that's a major problem because it affects your other thoughts, emotions, physical feelings and actions.

BUT the solution is staring you in the face: you created that thought by repeating it so YOU can weaken it by putting something else in its place. You can replace the negative pathways with new, positive thoughts.

BODY BOOST

Think about: who do you know that you admire? Is it their looks or something else that you so admire? Would you rather be admired and respected for what you've done or what you look like? Keep focusing on this. What do you want to be known for? How will you make that happen?

Let me illustrate this. (In the resources at the end of this chapter, you'll find a link to my Pathways Powerpoint which demonstrates this.) Imagine you're going for a walk on a grassy hill. You come to a point where the path disappears. You can see the place you've got to reach to meet the path again, but you have to choose how to get there. So, you choose your route and pick your way over the grass and stones and meet the path. Next day, you repeat the walk and you come to that same place. You have to choose your route again. You are most likely to choose the same route: the same things that made you choose it will probably apply today; and it's a little familiar now and it worked yesterday. Next day: the same. And so on. Each time you take that route, you're more likely to take it the next time. You're really familiar with it now – and you can probably even see the pathway.

You've created the pathway. You'll probably go on using it. Forever.

Unless … you decide not to. One day, you could take a different route. It would be more difficult, but you could do it. And when you've done it once, you could do it again. And again. And gradually that first path would become weaker, fainter. Eventually you'd barely remember it. It wouldn't disappear entirely, but it wouldn't dictate your route any more.

It's the same with a negative thought. If you've had that thought hundreds or thousands of times it's not going to be easy to have a different thought, but you can do it, especially with someone helping you.

You can replace the negative thoughts in your mind. And, if you do, you've just done your own CBT. Well done!

Summing up

Although you might need expert help, for example a course of CBT, there are some ways you can help yourself think along more positive lines. CBT is a simple, practical therapy which involves identifying and understanding the negative thinking patterns that hinder positive self-esteem and body image. Low self-esteem and negative body image encourage us to have negative behaviours that prevent us making the most of ourselves and our lives but CBT retrains our minds so that we can grasp the opportunities in front of us.

Our thoughts are just habits and habits can be broken. Sometimes we can do this by ourselves but sometimes we need some professional help.

RESOURCES FOR THIS CHAPTER

ONLINE

The NHS (UK) has apps and tools and some are free: https://apps.beta.nhs.uk/category/mental_health/ Choose one that's right for your age. The NHS also provides 'Guided self-help' where you don't have full-scale CBT but work through a self-help book with the guidance of a trained person. Ask your GP.

Books on Prescription – books chosen by experts to direct you towards good mental health and mindsets: https://reading-well.org.uk/books/books-on-prescription/young-people-s-mental-health/stress

How CBT works: https://www.nhs.uk/conditions/cognitive-behavioural-therapy-cbt/how-it-works/

The Pathways Powerpoint on my website: go to www.nicolamorgan.com and put 'pathways' in the search box.

BOOKS

Fiction

Am I Normal Yet? by Holly Bourne has the main character going through therapy

Non-fiction

The CBT Workbook by Dr Stephanie Fitzgerald

Section One
SUMMING UP

We've come to the end of the *All in the Mind* section. Now you know all the many pressures that go towards how we see our bodies and whether we have a negative or positive body image. You've seen how body image can be powerfully affected by what you look at, including all the 'perfect' models and images you see online and in all media. You've seen how in most media-dominated cultures nowadays there's a thin ideal for women and a muscled ideal for men, but that in previous times and in some cultures the ideal has been for much more body fat for both men and women.

You now understand how gender may come into it and that people whose assigned gender doesn't match their identity might struggle as their bodies change into an adult man's or woman's. And you've seen extreme problems, such as Body Dysmorphic Disorder and eating disorders.

I hope you've followed some of the suggested Body Boosts. If you have, your thinking and mindset will have already started to change. You'll have seen a far bigger range of normal body shapes than you'd see if you only follow a narrow body type online and you'll have a much more accurate, realistic picture of what normal people look like when they've not been artificially enhanced by photo-editing software or cosmetic procedures.

I hope that in your mind you're already more positive about your body, more respectful of it and more kind to yourself.

But your brilliant body doesn't just need your respect: it needs you to look after it and make it the best it can be. That's what the rest of the book is about...

Section Two

MAKING YOUR BODY BRILLIANT

When I talk about physical and mental health, I use the image of a four-legged table, the 'Table of Well-being'. The four legs are:

1. Food and water

2. Exercise

3. Sleep

4. Relaxation

My simple theory is that if we look after all four of these things as well as we can, we'll have better physical health and mental well-being than if we don't. You know that if one leg in a real four-legged table breaks, the whole table collapses. It's the same with this table: you have to look after all the legs.

Mental and physical well-being are closely connected: if you're physically unwell or weak, it affects your mental state, and if you don't look after your mind, your physical health suffers.

This doesn't mean we all have to be 100 per cent well all the time – that isn't possible. Everyone gets illnesses sometimes, even if they do everything right. And some people start off with a physical health problem or a disability, or have other really big hurdles along the way, so some people have much bigger challenges to well-being.

But everyone, regardless of problems, can take steps to have the best possible physical and mental health. Our choices do make a difference and are definitely worth the effort. And sometimes it's no effort! Many of the things I'll talk about in this section are about pleasure, fun, excitement, achievement and satisfaction. Being well is not boring!

chapter eleven

FEED YOUR BRILLIANT BODY

Food is fuel. Without fuel, there's no energy. If you want your body to work well – or work at all – it needs enough energy, which only comes from eating enough food. If you don't eat enough, or what you eat doesn't have the right range of nutrients, your body can't function well. You'll find your concentration suffers and your muscles are weak. You'll also be more vulnerable to illnesses.

One part of your body requires a *lot* of fuel: your brain. The brain is very energy-hungry, more than any other organ, using around 20 per cent of the total energy your body requires. The fuel that the brain uses is glucose, which your body obtains from the food you eat. Glucose is a type of sugar and is made when our body breaks down foods containing carbohydrates. These are a really important part of the diet and include starchy carbohydrates, such as potatoes, pasta, rice, cereals and bread.

The energy our food contains is measured in calories. (There are some different measurements, such as kilojoules, but let's just stick with calories.) We need to consume enough calories, otherwise our body and brain won't work well and other processes will be affected, such as cell repair, hair growth and immune system, which all require enough calories and also all the nutrients in food.

BODY BOOST

Choose an inspiring cookbook, website or magazine. Spend time finding a recipe you'd love to try. Do it! Sometimes it won't work – I'm a very confident cook but I still make mistakes sometimes.

Young people particularly need plenty of calories because you're growing and changing, and that takes energy even if you're not actually *doing* anything. Each new, growing or repairing cell needs energy, as well as nutrients, such as proteins, fats, vitamins and minerals.

But what if you feel you're growing too fast and you want to slow it down? Restricting food is very dangerous and may hinder healthy development instead of actual growth. For example, you're currently developing bone strength and thickness that will help prevent breaks later in life. This requires calcium and vitamin D. Restricting food reduces the amount of vitamins and minerals in your diet and can affect hair, skin, mood, sleep, exercise performance and immune function (how well you fight disease).

→ HOW MANY CALORIES?

Please don't count calories. Most food packages display estimated calorie contents, but adding them up is not recommended, especially for young people. There are some people who might be advised to focus on calories, usually because they need to eat more, rather than fewer; or because a doctor or dietitian has specified a certain number of calories as being appropriate for them. For everyone else, calorie counting risks an unhealthy lifestyle and attitude, and introduces the problems of dieting, which I'll explain in a moment.

You'll know if you're consuming enough because you'll have enough energy to do the things you want to do. Your brain and body will work well and you won't feel hungry – except before a meal, when you're supposed to feel hungry!

If you're more active, you need more calories to stay healthy. And there's a difference in calorie needs for average females compared with average males, and how much children and teenagers need compared to adults. Some individuals need more energy than others because they are more active, or have more or less muscle, or a bigger or smaller frame. All this makes a difference.

THE TROUBLE WITH DIETING

Dieting means restricting food intake in some way. It might mean consuming less overall or eliminating or reducing certain foods. In the short term making radical changes to your diet may result in weight loss, but it is very hard to maintain and often weight is regained. Repeated dieting 'failures' then risk increasing your body dissatisfaction and self-esteem.

 "I did think life would be perfect once I got thin. It wasn't. I was physically lighter but life's difficulties weighed the same."
Hazel

This is how people end up 'yo-yo dieting'. And this is what so often happens. If dieting worked, the diet industry wouldn't be so huge. The diet industry is huge because people have to keep going on diets, over and over again.

Let me give you a statistic that might make you think twice about dieting: according to the (Canadian) National Eating Disorder Information Centre[28], 'Adolescent girls who diet are at 324 per cent higher risk for becoming obese than those who do not diet.' Dieting is also a predictor of eating disorders and linked to disordered eating.

Unfortunately, the pressure to diet is all around us. In the US, UK, Australia and many European countries, we keep being told that we have an obesity problem; parents may be informed when a school believes a child should lose weight; health messages talk frequently about the calories in certain products; guilt is regularly associated with eating chocolate or cake or desserts; and parents very often talk about their own weight: 'Oh, I must lose a few pounds before the summer holidays' or 'Oh no! I've put on a kilo this week! I'll need to cut out bread for a week.'

So, over and over again, you are receiving messages about food and weight. The vital thing to remember is: you're growing! You need a variety of food and enough of it, otherwise your body and brain won't work so well.

"I've tried to lose weight and exercise at weekends. It's exhausting and time-consuming."
Bella 15

For nearly all young people, dieting harms their body. It disrupts the necessary hunger/fullness cues, affects the body's metabolism and can lead to a damaging cycle of disordered eating. After losing weight, most people gain more than they lost. If you have a desire to lose weight, *always consult your doctor.*

28 http://nedic.ca/know-facts/statistics

When online, never click on adverts that promote weight loss: they're trying to sell you something and don't care about your health. They don't know you, your weight or health issues. Never take slimming pills, which don't lead to long-term weight loss and can be dangerous; trust your appetite; and never restrict food – certainly never to a level that means you're hungry, dizzy, snappy or lacking concentration.

You want to enjoy a pleasurable and relaxed attitude to food and movement, and be strong and fit, not weak and always aspiring to be thinner.

BUT WHAT IF I AM OVERWEIGHT? SHOULDN'T I LOSE SOME?

Only your doctor or another relevantly qualified person can tell you if you are an unhealthy weight for your height and age. The scales themselves cannot tell you and your eyes certainly can't; nor can anyone around you (see chapter one). There is a wide range of weights and waist sizes which are perfectly healthy, usually measured by BMI (Body Mass Index) and then plotted on special charts for different age groups. But even using a BMI chart doesn't tell you enough.

If a medically-qualified person who has examined you says your BMI is too high, they will help you achieve a healthier weight for your age, under expert supervision. But it shouldn't be called a 'diet': it should be a new, healthy lifestyle, full of wonderful foods that you like, exercise that will make you feel great, and loads of new tips and habits that will make your body brilliant.

As well as the personal medical advice from your doctor or dietitian, you might also use online advice. If so, only use well-established and official organisations that promote healthy lifestyles, not ones that promote skinniness. I'll repeat what I said above, as it's so important: avoid adverts for weight loss and don't take slimming pills. And never restrict food to a level that means you're hungry, dizzy, snappy or lacking concentration.

> *"I'm a bit worried about my weight, though I know I have a nice body shape and good proportions. I am worried because I like eating so much. I do squats and sit-ups every day and run around the park or go to the gym. I was super-fit in primary but now I've put on a lot of weight and it makes me really anxious."*
> **Aquilat, 14**

! AUTHOR NOTE: DON'T STOP ENJOYING FOOD! FOOD MAKES YOU STRONG AND HEALTHY AND WE ARE WIRED TO ENJOY IT. RESPECT YOUR BODY AND WHAT IT NEEDS.

Instead of focusing on weight loss, think about what healthy behaviours you can adopt, such as being more active, joining a group activity, having less screentime, eating more fruits and vegetables. But remember that being 'slim' is not the aim: being strong, healthy and fit is the aim.

Weight is complicated: don't deal with it on your own.

How to eat well

Here are my tips. I've had them checked by a dietitian, but it's still general advice and if you have any particular health, weight or anxiety issues around food it's really important that you follow your own doctor's or dietitian's advice.

Love food

Although food is fuel and provides the energy and nutrients for our body and brain to work brilliantly, it's even more than that. Food can – and should – give us pleasure. Humans, like all animals, have evolved to enjoy the tastes of certain foods. Feeling hungry is important because it reminds us to eat and liking the foods we eat is important because it makes us eat what we need to thrive.

How our brains are wired goes back to times when food wasn't plentiful so we didn't have the opportunity to over-eat. But modern humans have two important 'problems': first, for most people in wealthier communities, there's much more food than our ancestors had and it's easy to get at any time of day, so we often eat more than we need. And often what's cheapest and most easily available isn't the most nutritious food. We ignore our important hunger or fullness cues and just eat because it's there.

Second, many of us have guilt about food. We often feel ashamed when we put on weight – because of all the messages promoting thinness and suggesting that being overweight is because of greed or laziness – so we try to curb our natural desire to eat sweet or fatty food. And when we fail, we tend to feel guilty.

"For me, feeling comfortable in my body is about eating healthily and exercising through sports that I love. I love my food, which used to make me worry about over-eating but when I realised that food does not mean weight this helped me enjoy eating and doing sport to make me healthy and happy in my body."
Cally, 16

So, we are wired to love high-calorie foods because we need calories to survive and thrive and this wiring comes from a time when calories weren't so easy to find; but, surrounded by so many temptations, some of us may feel anxious or guilty when we enjoy these pleasures. It's a tricky balance: knowledge about healthy eating can too easily tip into harmful negative guilty feelings and a negative attitude to food. And that negative attitude often makes food become the controlling enemy instead of the nourishing friend it should be. This is why government and school 'healthy eating' campaigns can often have the opposite effect: by creating guilt around certain foods, they make those foods more tempting, and they allow us to ignore the importance of eating what our instinct tells us we need.

How can we eat well in the modern world when our brains are wired for an ancient one? Read on...

Build a big list of wonderful foods you love

Try not to think of them as either 'good' or 'bad'. Think of the ones that it's great to fill up on because they're going to give you energy and strength and health; and others that are better as add-on treats. Make your list as big and varied as you can.

Eat a variety

No single food has every nutrient so no food (or food type) is enough on its own. You don't need to learn the complicated facts about what each contains: just eat the biggest variety possible and you'll automatically have the best diet.

One extra way to ensure you're eating a variety of nutrients is to vary the natural colours: the things that naturally make foods different colours tend to relate to different nutrients. Think of carrots and oranges;

tomatoes and strawberries; blueberries and aubergines; peas, broccoli, spinach; cauliflowers; bananas. (Foods that are artificially coloured don't count!)

Another type of variety involves the different food groups. So, try to choose items from **all of these over the period of a day:**

- ❦ **Carbohydrates:** pasta, rice, potato, bread – have some of these at every meal
- ❦ **Protein:** especially eggs, fish, poultry, beans, pulses, grains, nuts and seeds
- ❦ **Dairy:** milk, yogurt, cheese (and there are non-cow or non-animal varieties, which you can research for different benefits) – aim for around three servings a day for strong bones
- ❦ **Fruit and vegetables**
- ❦ **Fats:** oils from plants, such as olives, nuts and seeds are great. Avocadoes and oily fish, such as mackerel and salmon are rich in healthy oils.

You'll find resources to help you balance these groups at the end of the chapter.

BODY BOOST

Have you eaten a rainbow today? Think about all the foods you've eaten: if you put them all on one plate would there be all the colours of the rainbow? Whichever colours are missing, make a point of adding them in tomorrow or the next day.

"People get bullied for curves or for being skinny. When someone is bullied they might use food to make themselves fatter or thinner but they still get bullied."
Shaniqua

Ignore extremes, fads and restrictive habits

Every now and then a fad or theory comes along and someone – often a celebrity or other individual without proper training in nutrition but with a book or product to sell – tells us to eat or avoid particular foods or eat in particular ways or specific combinations. Take these with a pinch of salt (not literally!). You might hear that such-and-such (often an expensive item) is the new wonder-food and should be added to everything. Or that something is very bad for us and must be avoided. These ideas are often based on one small study or an unproven theory. Many studies contradict each other, too. People are always looking for magic routes to health, but restricting food in almost any way is not recommended until it's so well-established that it's government policy. Even then, what is right for an adult's diet may not be right for a teenager's or child's diet.

Cutting out items from our diets risks our overall diet and health. For example, a few people decide only to eat raw food, but this is not recommended by dietitians because it means restricting and analysing foods too much and you are likely to be eating a nutritionally deficient diet. Raw food can be wonderful, but so can cooked food. Different foods respond better to being raw or cooked.

There are various other systems which claim to be healthy approaches to food – 'clean eating' is one example – but again they are riskily restrictive, especially for young people, as you are growing, needing a wide range of nutrients and enough energy to function and develop.

So, the best advice is: eat a wide range of foods because they'll all give you something. Eat what you feel your body needs. Be moderate. Don't seek magic answers or become a guinea pig by testing out some new idea that hasn't stood the test of time and proper, repeated research.

Understand about processed foods

There's a lot of talk in the media about 'processed food' and much of it is negative. But there's nothing at all wrong with many processed foods and in fact there are various methods of processing that help keep foods fresh. For example, freezing and canning can be great ways of preserving nutrients and many factory processes have no negative effects. Categorising a food according to whether it has been processed ignores whether that food is high in nutrients. For example, wholemeal bread is a processed food and yet is part of a healthy diet.

There is some evidence of a link between obesity and eating *a lot* of highly-processed food (as opposed to lightly-processed) and also some evidence linking a highly-processed diet to serious illnesses, such as cancer and heart disease, but we don't know if this means those foods cause the problems or if they are linked in some other way. The British Nutrition Foundation's website helps explain this in more detail. You'll find links at the end of the chapter.

The current expert advice is that highly-processed foods – such as processed meats, pies and confectionery with many different ingredients – are better occupying a smaller part of our diet. As with pretty much everything, moderation rather than obsession is the key.

Try new tastes

Our tastes change as we get older and as we try new
things. It's good to widen your taste because that gives
you more options and more pleasure. Often, particularly
with a strong taste, we don't like it the first time but, if
we try it again, or maybe have it cooked differently, we
might. Also, most things don't taste exactly the same each time:
for example, different varieties of olives or tomatoes or cheese
can taste very different, so, just because you didn't like one
cheese doesn't mean you don't like any cheese.

BODY BOOST

Think of a food you've never eaten.
Discuss with whoever chooses the meals in your
family and see if you could try it. Maybe each
family member could pick something new each week?
No pressure to like it, though! It could be: olives;
a fish you've never had; one of those exotic/
weird-looking fruits; sushi. Challenge your family
that each week one meal will be something
you've never tried.

Taste is about pleasure and it's purely personal. But it does take
practice too, and it's practice that's worth doing so that you can
have a great relationship with food and more enjoyment. Eating
in a restaurant or at other people's houses can be very difficult if
you have a narrow range of likes.

Get cooking

One of the best ways to enjoy food is to cook it yourself or join in the family cooking. When I was a teenager, I made a mean savoury rice, adding all sorts of interesting things and developing my taste-buds along the way. No one else in my family was allowed to make it!

It's also one of the best ways to know what's in your food. It gives you power over an incredibly basic human need: the food that fuels our bodies. It's a set of skills you'll find useful forever.

Get growing stuff

Growing things to eat is one of the most satisfying hobbies. You don't need a big garden: it's amazing what you can grow in a tiny garden, in pots on a sunny patio, on a balcony or even on a windowsill. What you can grow will depend on the climate where you live and even a few hundred kilometres north or south will make quite a difference, but there are things you can grow even in colder countries.

Almost anything can be grown in a pot, though obviously some things would need a big container. Some plants can grow up a pole or trellis, taking up much less ground space.

BODY BOOST

Hide healthy ingredients that you don't like inside foods you do. For example, any of these can be inserted into loads of recipes or meals and you'll never know: linseeds, oats, lentils, beans; any of these things puréed: spinach, tomato, berries, kale; pretty much anything can make a fabulous smoothie and you'll never know what was in it!

If you're interested in doing anything like this, research plants that will work in your location – and that you'd like to eat! Look for how to grow: herbs to put on pizzas, in risottos, pasta sauces, salads and casseroles and even sandwiches; micro-greens on a sunny window-sill; a tomato plant in a pot or hanging basket; a chilli plant – just one can produce around a hundred chillies and you could then make chilli jam to eat with cheese or cold meats and give it away as presents; things that can grow up a pole or trellis, such as beans, peas, tomatoes, squash and cucumbers (in a greenhouse or conservatory unless you live in a very warm place.)

Food with friends

Food brings people together. It doesn't have to be a meal out: you can have friends round or go to someone's house. Why not ask if you can have friends over and either cook together or you cook for them?

If a whole meal feels too ambitious, how about making a cake at the weekend and inviting friends round after school on Monday or Tuesday? (Most cakes keep for several days.) Or invite them round for a pizza-making session? Making pizza is fun and easy and the result is very tasty.

BODY BOOST

Go nuts! Nuts are fabulously nutritious (as long as you're not allergic, of course) and different ones have different nutrients so vary them.

Or plan a meal where each of your friends brings one dish – salads or dips for the ones who are less confident. Start a foodie supper club: once a month you take turns to host the meal, each person bringing one dish; you could have themed nights, such as Indian, Spanish tapas, Christmas, American, vegetarian or vegan. Remember that some people will have a negative relationship with food, either having very narrow tastes, being afraid of new things, or being afraid of putting on weight, so it's important not to add any pressure. And do let people be open about things they really don't like or can't eat because of an allergy. It doesn't matter if someone doesn't eat a lot or doesn't like something. What's important is that you all come together to enjoy each other's company around food.

Celebrate with food

Birthdays, feast days, religious festivals, weddings and celebrations of an event, such as the end of term or a graduation, all these are associated with having richer and even more delicious, indulgent food than usual. Food is part of celebration. It always has been, in every culture.

BODY BOOST

Go out for an ice-cream or cake with a friend. Enjoy it! Your body deserves and needs treats sometimes.

I am unusual because I dislike most cake but I was always taught that if it was someone's birthday and there was a cake, I ought to have a bit, because to say 'no' would be rude. It would be like saying 'No, I don't want to celebrate with you'. Although I don't like the idea of 'should' or 'shouldn't' being associated with food, I do think it's good to see

food as something to share, something sociable, something that connects us. So, I'll always eat a bit, to join the celebration.

If you have any kind of disordered eating, you will find it difficult to see food as a celebration. You may see it as an enemy, something to conquer and control. You may feel scared of rich food – the cream, chocolate and butter that so often form part of feast food – and you may feel guilty when you've had some of it. You may even be feeling anxious as you read this section. If that's how you feel, do make sure you're getting expert help so that you can have a happier relationship with food (and take another look at chapter nine: Eating Disorders and Self-harm).

Being able to enjoy celebration food is important, something that is natural and human, sociable and rewarding, and something that you deserve.

WHAT ABOUT WATER?

We also need water, even though it has no energy value. Our bodies are made of around 70 per cent water and we lose this through sweating, breathing and going to the toilet, so we have to keep water levels up by drinking. We need more water when we are hot, unwell, or when we've done exercise. But how much? And what sort? And aren't all drinks made of water?

How much?

Being thirsty is a signal to drink. Keep water with you if possible and aim to drink enough, so that you don't feel thirsty. Drink more in hot weather or when doing physical exercise.

Health organisations suggest we aim for at least six glasses of liquid a day in cool weather and eight glasses in warm weather or during activity. But this *includes* water in food and other drinks, so it needn't all be pure water. (Most foods contain a lot of water. For example, an apple is about 85 per cent water.)

What about other drinks?

All drinks are mostly water, but they don't all do an equal job of keeping our fluid level up. So, it matters where we get our water. The ideal is plain water. Some other drinks are fine, but we need to know the differences. Here are the facts, and I've tried to put the drinks in order of health, with the better choices first:

🍀 Milk – great for most people; as well as water content, it has many nutrients, including protein, calcium (for bones and teeth) and vitamins. Some people don't want to or can't drink cow (dairy) milk, but there are alternatives – such as sheep or goat's milk, and non-animal options, such as oat, almond, coconut or soya – but these are often expensive and there are environmental or ethical questions over some. Each different type of milk contains different nutrients, so replacing dairy milk with any other variety does not replicate the nutrients of dairy milk. I suggest you do some research about the milk you drink or want to drink so you can choose well.

🍀 Fruit or herbal teas and other caffeine-free teas – good alternatives to part of your water needs.

🍀 Fruit juice and smoothies – all contain acid and sugar which harm our teeth, so we shouldn't drink too much.

🍃 Diluting fruit juice or 'squash' – these may have a lot of sugar, artificial sweeteners and artificial colours, all of which aren't ideal. Don't consume too often and do dilute as much as possible. Choose low or no-sugar varieties to protect your teeth.

🍃 Caffeine – in coffee, most teas and some energy drinks and cola. The UK Food Standards Agency suggests that moderate amounts are safe and the evidence is that teenagers respond to caffeine in the same way as adults do: it generally has a wakening effect (which we would want to avoid in the hours before bed) and some people find that drinking a lot of it makes them feel jittery and uncomfortable.

🍃 Fizzy (carbonated) drinks – for occasional treats only, especially those that contain lots of sugar, as they are bad for teeth. They are habit-forming, too.

🍃 Energy drinks – avoid these very high-caffeine, high-sugar drinks that also contain other stimulants and additives. Don't take my word for it: do your research, ignoring the claims of the manufacturers who want your money! These drinks are very powerful 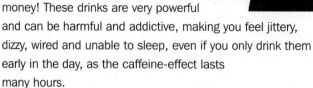 and can be harmful and addictive, making you feel jittery, dizzy, wired and unable to sleep, even if you only drink them early in the day, as the caffeine-effect lasts many hours.

🍃 Alcohol – does NOT count towards water intake because it is dehydrating and brings other problems, especially for young people. Combining alcohol with energy drinks is a terrible idea. You want your brain to work well: alcohol does not do this.

What happens if we don't drink enough?

Symptoms of being dehydrated include headaches, dizziness, loss of concentration and irritability. You will also notice that your urine is darker. Drink water and you'll notice an instant improvement to how you feel. Keeping your fluid levels up will help you focus and feel better.

Can we drink too much water?

Yes, it's possible. Our blood needs the right balance of minerals, salt and chemicals. If you drink much too much water, you dilute your blood and change that balance. Having too much water in your body is called hyponatremia, a rare but occasionally fatal condition, where sodium levels fall dangerously low.

Don't obsess about drinking enough; for example, don't fill your water bottle as soon as you've finished it. The only times you need to drink more than the recommended 6–8 glasses a day (*including* water from food and other drinks) is if you're sweating a lot from heat or exercise. Drink when you're thirsty or you haven't had a drink for a while.

There are a few illnesses – diabetes is one – where unusual thirst is a symptom, so if you're frequently thirsty when you've not been exercising and the weather isn't hot, a doctor should check you out.

CHECK YOUR SALT INTAKE

Salt makes us thirsty. You'll notice this when you eat something like crisps or salted peanuts. This happens because salt removes water from everything around it. If you put a bowl of salt in a damp room, the salt sucks moisture from the air and becomes damp. If you put salt in your body, it reduces the water levels in your blood, making your blood thicker. The body balances this by making us feel thirsty so we drink enough water. Clever!

We need *some* salt, but not too much. If we eat lots of salty things we often crave more. The trouble is that many popular foods are high in salt: crisps, most savoury snacks, processed food, takeaways, ready meals. And it's not just foods that *taste* salty: many varieties of baked beans and savoury sauces have lots of salt, masked by lots of sugar. Soy sauce is very salty so go easy on that.

Salt makes our food tasty (as sugar does), but we can train our taste-buds to prefer less salty food. And you'll do your brilliant body a big favour that way. Make things tasty by adding lemon or lime juice, herbs or pepper. I think most food, if it's fresh enough and cooked nicely, needs no salt. Exceptions are probably eggs and potatoes, but you'll find that cayenne pepper peps up an egg, while olive oil and chilli are fantastic on a baked potato.

"When I was 11, I was teased for being chubby. My 'friends' would tell me they had been talking about me behind my back and calling me fat. Hearing these things from people who I thought I was close to really hurt. I used to beg my mum to help me diet and let me join her when she went to the gym. I'm still very self-conscious about my body, but I'm learning to love it because of school talks about body image and realising that everyone's bodies are different. My message is to surround yourself with people who love you for you, not what you look like."

Sarah, 16

Your body loves a wide variety of foods!

Summing up

There are three important things to remember about food for your brilliant body: first, you need enough of it because it's the only way your body can work properly, including growing new cells so that you have good skin and hair and nails, and so that your brain works as well as it can.

Second, the more variety we have the more likely our diet is to give us everything we need. Following fads or unproven theories or becoming obsessed about what we should and shouldn't eat is not the way to a brilliant body and positive body image.

Third, food is not only fuel but also pleasure. I don't ask you to eat anything you don't like. I'd love you to try everything – and more than once, because it's common not to like things at first – but if you dislike something you don't have to eat it. Aim to find loads of fantastic foods and flavours you love and eat a wide range of them, feeling positive about your choices that will feed your body and brain.

Feel good about food and food will do you good. As waiters say in restaurants: Enjoy!

RESOURCES FOR THIS CHAPTER

ONLINE

The brain and energy:
www.scientificamerican.com/article/why-does-the-brain-need-s/

Teenagers need more calories than adults:
www.healthychildren.org/English/ages-stages/teen/nutrition/Pages/A-Teenagers-Nutritional-Needs.aspx

www.nhlbi.nih.gov/health/educational/wecan/downloads/calreqtips.pdf

How to balance the five food groups:
Australia: https://healthy-kids.com.au/food-nutrition/5-food-groups/

UK: www.nhs.uk/live-well/eat-well/the-eatwell-guide/

US: www.usda.gov/media/blog/2017/09/26/back-basics-all-about-myplate-food-groups

The British Nutrition Foundation's information on processed foods: www.nutrition.org.uk/bnfevents/events/125-nutritioninthenews/headlines.html and www.nutrition.org.uk/nutritioninthenews/headlines/ultraprocessedfoods.html

Information about various drinks: www.nutrition.org.uk/attachments/article/429/Healthy%20hydration%20for%20adults.pdf

The problem with energy drinks: www.eatingwell.com/article/278049/10-common-energy-drink-ingredients-what-you-need-to-know/

Recipe sites for teenagers:
BBC: www.bbcgoodfood.com/howto/guide/recipes-teenagers

Martha Stewart: www.marthastewart.com/1505773/13-super-easy-meals-teens-can-make-themselves

DIY Projects for teens: https://diyprojectsforteens.com/diy-recipes-teens/

chapter twelve

FIND YOUR EXERCISE

Are you tired of hearing that exercise is good for you and that you should do more? It can be a very annoying message if you don't enjoy exercise, or you're very unfit, ill or disabled and think exercise isn't something you can do or enjoy. People (and websites) can sound very bossy, unsympathetic and elitist, only seeming to talk to those lucky enough already to enjoy exercise.

I want to avoid bossiness because I understand how annoying and pointless it is. I have always struggled to enjoy exercise: I hate being hot and sweaty, can't bear competitive sport (watching or participating) and find any kind of team or doubles sport very stressful. I'm self-conscious and don't like doing activities in front of other people. Added to all that, I've a history of bad joints since I was about ten. And I find it hard to fit exercise into a busy life.

So, I have every reason for finding it difficult and for sympathising if you do.

"I'm not naturally sporty so I need to find exercise I like so I can be healthy. Cycling and running are good for that and make my legs stronger."
Nana Kwame, 14

But, I've also read masses of research and know that exercise really benefits health, physically and mentally. The trouble is that, if we don't like it, we probably won't do it for long enough to find those benefits, so it's essential to find exercise we can *enjoy*. This might involve trying several different things and certainly involves perseverance, but I believe there's an exercise everyone can enjoy, whatever their fitness level, ability, disability and personality.

Before we can be motivated to find the right exercise, we need to believe the benefits.

 "Feeling good on the inside is so much more important than what is seen on the outside. The release of feel good endorphins when exercising, in particular when dancing to music, encourages us to associate feeling good with being active. Healthier attitudes are generally easy to achieve through fun activity, which is why I am so passionate about getting dance fitness as part of PE in schools for EVERY young person regardless of size, age, or ability."
Dame Darcey Bussell, DBE

→ How does exercise benefit us?

Note: if you have a medical condition, use your personal knowledge of it to decide which of these benefits might or might not apply to you. If you're not sure, ask your doctor.

Different activities do different things: some use particular muscles; some focus on heart and lungs. No single exercise or sport deals with everything. Benefits of various exercises include the following.

Healthy weight

As you know, this is not a book about losing weight, but exercise plays the major part in keeping within a healthy weight range. If you exercise too much, you'll risk harm, but some exercise on most days is a really good aim and will help you have a strong body and mind.

 "I do lots of exercise but I don't do it to make myself look a certain way but because I enjoy it and I believe it's helping my health in lots of ways."
Adam, 13

Stronger muscles and joints

For a healthy person without injuries or specific challenges, exercising helps build strong muscles to protect joints. You can run faster, lift more, throw further, feel stronger.

Lots of problems with joints, particularly knees and ankles, which have to carry our weight, are caused or worsened by weak muscles not supporting those joints. If you have problems or injuries affecting any joints, bones or muscles, it's important for a physiotherapist to show you the correct exercises to help strengthen muscles, tendons and ligaments. You shouldn't ignore pain. But simply stopping exercise is usually not the way to deal with joint problems: it's more complicated and does involve expert guided exercise.

BODY BOOST

Put on your favourite music and dance in your room. Practise your moves in front of a mirror.

Strong bones

'Impact' activities, such as jumping, running or gymnastics, strengthen the bones in our legs or arms. They help make bones 'denser' and less likely to fracture. It's much harder to build bone density when you're older, so doing this sort of exercise now is a great idea.

However, too much high impact exercise can cause damage. If you do a lot of running or jumping, ask your school PE teacher or a qualified sports trainer at your local community gym to check whether you're doing too much and to advise about building the right muscles to support your limbs.

Strong heart and lower 'resting heart rate'

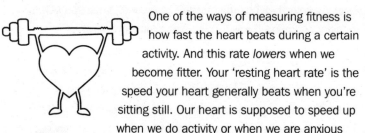

One of the ways of measuring fitness is how fast the heart beats during a certain activity. And this rate *lowers* when we become fitter. Your 'resting heart rate' is the speed your heart generally beats when you're sitting still. Our heart is supposed to speed up when we do activity or when we are anxious because we are about to perform in some way, but a healthy heart doesn't speed up more than necessary and returns to its resting rate quite quickly after you stop. 'Cardio' exercise (which you can keep up for a good amount of time, such as gentle jogging or fast walking, as opposed to sprinting) helps this.

Better complexion

When we exercise, we help more blood flow everywhere in our body, including the skin. Blood carries oxygen as well as nutrients, helping our skin to be healthy. Oxygen helps skin produce collagen, giving it natural elasticity. Your skin will look great after exercise. (Once the bright red appearance has gone!)

Less stress

People who exercise usually notice immediate stress-relieving benefits. There are several reasons: exercise makes your body produce chemicals called endorphins, the brain's natural feel-good chemicals; concentrating on the exercise can take your mind off your worries; and afterwards you have a sense of well-being and achievement. Even if the effect isn't immediate, most people who exercise will notice that they feel less stressed a bit later.

Better sleep

Although doing fast or vigorous exercise during the evening doesn't help sleep because it makes you alert, doing it earlier in the day, or slow exercise (such as yoga) in the evening, seems to improve sleep for most people.

Better mood

The endorphins your brain produces during exercise raise mood, making you feel more positive and giving a sense of achievement. Even if you didn't actually enjoy it while you were doing it, there's still the sense of *'Yay! I did that!'*

Research has looked at the value of exercise for people with depressive illnesses. The clear message is: it may be the last thing you feel like doing but, if you can do it, you won't regret it. You might need help to get motivated and find an activity you can manage, but it will be worth it. Keep reading and I'll share strategies for doing exercise when you really don't want to!

 "I do kayaking and swimming, which make me happy and I'm keen to improve my skills."
Maria, 15

It brings a sense of well-being when you start to notice that your body works better and is stronger and healthier; you might meet new friends; you'll learn something new; and you could really surprise yourself by enjoying it more than you imagined.

For some people with depression or anxiety, exercise becomes a life-saver. Of course, some people don't find the exercise that works for them and never get to experience the benefits, but it's really worth trying. You might need to persevere; you might make different attempts at different activities; and you might need help from a friend or group.

But if you don't try you'll never know.

FINDING AN ACTIVITY YOU CAN ENJOY

When I say 'enjoying' exercise, I don't mean you'll necessarily be ecstatic as you get out of bed on a cold morning, head to the local swimming pool and shiver in the changing rooms. I do not expect you to love the feeling of being out of breath and sweaty. Some people do enjoy those sensations but many don't!

BODY BOOST

If you dislike exercise, find a friend who feels the same: brainstorm ideas that you could do together or support each other with. Remember that it doesn't have to be competitive, difficult, or team-based.

For those, like me, who struggle with the unpleasant parts, what I mean by *enjoy* is the feeling that comes on the home stretch, or as you shower and change back into clean clothes, feeling proud, alert, your lungs bigger than they were, your heart lighter. I mean the smile on your face as you realise what you did, as you think about how you'll work better for the rest of the day. I mean the higher self-esteem, the actual feelings of happiness as you start to make your body even more brilliant each time. You'll only know what I mean if you experience it for yourself and it may not happen at first. Do keep at it!

 "I didn't like exercise when I was at school – it seemed so competitive and the teachers didn't like me because I wasn't good enough at it. So, for years I didn't do it, even though I knew I should. But now I swim three times a week and it gives me strength, health and an incredible feel-good factor every time. If I go first thing in the morning, it affects my whole day positively."
Caroline

HERE ARE MY TIPS FOR FINDING THE RIGHT EXERCISE FOR YOU:

🍀 **Know yourself:** will you prefer individual or team activities, competitive or non-competitive ones? Do you want to exercise with others or alone? Do you fancy quick exercise (running and football) or slow exercise (walking or yoga)? Do you need it to be over quickly, for example a quick walk, or do you have time for an afternoon of cricket or golf or an evening of gymnastics? Are you up for something completely new or do you want to stick with something easy or familiar?

🍀 **Be open to new ideas:** even things you don't think you'll like. Learning to run was completely unexpected for me: I'd always said it was something I didn't want to do. I'm so glad I did!

🍀 **Think local and do research:** use your public library, council website or school community to find local groups and clubs to inspire you. Whether it's indoor rock-climbing, open-water swimming, archery or anything else, there's something out there that could empower your brilliant body and mind.

🍀 **Download an exercise app:** plenty are free. A warning: don't connect to strangers, in case they know where you are, which is likely if you've added your location to the settings.

🍀 **Look for free workouts online:** if you have space, you could exercise without leaving home. Always stop if you have any pain, and if the pain persists get it checked out.

Get support: even if you want to exercise alone, you can still be part of a group. Some friends could set up an online group and encourage each other. Be careful that it's for support, not competition, unless competition is what you want. Don't be persuaded to overdo it. You need the support of similar people.

Don't aim too high: if you're not used to exercise, keep targets manageable, otherwise you won't enjoy it. The running programme I used (Couch to 5k) works well for beginner runners, because it starts from almost nothing and moves you forward gradually. Each target is manageable.

Exercise in your room: if you don't want to get undressed in front of others, don't, or arrive ready changed and pull on a tracksuit at the end so you can shower and change at home.

Forget the word 'exercise' and think of 'activity': gardening, vacuuming or cleaning for your parents, sweeping the yard or mowing the grass, posting a parcel for a neighbour, shopping, building a treehouse, cycling, climbing a tree, playing any game with your friends that involves not sitting still. Going for a walk is great, too: walk at a speed that raises your heart rate a bit so that you can talk, but not sing!

Put on your favourite music and dance: dancing is terrific exercise. Use blue-tooth headphones if you want to be private.

"I am very confident about my body image. Being a hockey player opens my eyes so I see that there is so much physical differentiation among both girls and boys. Some may be firm and muscly and others speedy and thin, but they are talented and both shapes are accepted in the hockey world just as they should be in normal life."

Sophie, 16

EXERCISING WITH A DISABILITY

If you have a disability, you know far better than I do what the options are. There are options, though, even though I understand that they will be restricted. People with significant physical disabilities can still use their bodies in an active way, improving their heart health, mood and the strength of whichever parts of their body they can exercise.

Online, the organisations that support your particular condition will have lots of suggestions. Your local health centre, library and sports centre will offer a range of options. And your doctors and therapists will also want to help. The Paralympians inspire us as to what is possible, but no one expects you to do what they do, just as no one expects an able-bodied person to reach the levels of Olympians, just because they choose to do some exercise.

It's about doing what you can and what you'll enjoy. And respecting your body enough to want to make it even more brilliant so that it can work for you.

WARNINGS

Too much exercise can damage your mental and physical health. As I've mentioned already, people with eating disorders or a very negative body image often over-exercise (see chapter nine).

After you've exercised, eat something; don't exercise because you've eaten something. If you find you're wanting to exercise because you just ate something and you plan to burn off calories, this is a dangerous way of thinking. Please talk to a trusted adult or doctor if this describes you.

Also, check that your exercise isn't compulsive. Are you frustrated when you can't attend a regular session? Do you miss out on fun and sociable activities because you simply must exercise? Are you driven to keep doing more, or to make your sessions longer and harder? Even if you are eating plenty and your body weight is normal, get help, as this compulsion could be part of an eating disorder.

"I personally think it's healthy to be skinny and toned or muscular. I try to eat healthily and exercise every day and I am happy with how my body looks, though I'm always trying to lose weight."
Ella, 15

> ! AUTHOR NOTE: IF YOU'RE NATURALLY SLIM, THAT'S FINE, BUT TRYING TO BE 'SKINNY' ISN'T HEALTHY AND THERE ARE MENTAL AND PHYSICAL RISKS ATTACHED. REMEMBER THAT GENUINELY EATING HEALTHILY MEANS EATING ENOUGH. BE CAREFUL NOT TO RESTRICT FOODS OR OBSESS ABOUT WEIGHT OR SHAPE. FEED YOUR BODY AND MIND.

Exercising too much can also damage your joints, especially as you are not yet fully grown. Teenagers and children cannot safely put their body through the type of exercise that might be fine for an adult. Young athletes need special attention from a qualified coach with training in sports science to make sure they don't overdo things, even if training for serious competitions.

If you have any medical conditions, or if you are overweight or underweight, you should check with your doctor first. Your doctor will probably be delighted for you to be active, but only they can know if what you're planning is a good idea.

There are some very rare conditions that can cause sudden death in an apparently fit young person who takes part in vigorous sport. Many sports clubs now offer screening for these conditions. The risk is very small but the screening is simple and you may want to get checked out. Talk to your club or check online advice from the charity, CRY (Cardiac Arrest in the Young).

If you're looking for ideas online, choose ones aimed at your age. If you do an online search for, for example, 'pilates for teens' or 'yoga for teens', you'll find loads of great (and often free) ways to learn the techniques you need.

BODY BOOST

Choose sports and hobbies that suit your fitness level and body shape. There are so many options to choose from: martial arts, football, hockey, scouting, geocaching, dance...

Summing up

We all have different attitudes to exercise and sport, as well as different abilities and challenges. But the science is so clear: exercise brings physical and mental benefits, immediate benefits as well as longer term ones. It's just as important as eating, sleeping and enjoying great food. With food, everyone will like different foods and it's important to go with our tastes but also try new things. Same with exercise.

Some people find exercise really hard to get into but with knowledge, a bit of perseverance and imagination, you can find activities that you can enjoy, even if the enjoyment only comes afterwards, as your heart-rate returns to normal and you bask in the glow of satisfaction of knowing that you did something that made your body and mind a little bit more brilliant.

Try not to be irritated when people tell you to exercise: it really is a vital part of looking after and respecting your body. If it's harder for you than for others, rise to that great challenge: you can do it!

RESOURCES FOR THIS CHAPTER

ONLINE

Benefits: https://teens.webmd.com/benefits-of-exercise#1

Exercise and stress: www.mayoclinic.org/healthy-lifestyle/stress-management/in-depth/exercise-and-stress/art-20044469

For teenage girls: www.askdrmanny.com/8-great-exercises-keep-teenage-girls-fit/

This Girl Can – media campaign to encourage girls to take up sports: www.thisgirlcan.co.uk/

For boys – on building muscle safely (but note that even a good medical site can contain adverts and links to sites that may not have good advice for your age): https://teens.webmd.com/boys/features/building-muscle-in-teen-boys#1

Core muscles: https://plankpose.com/core-muscles/

This video explains quite well how to engage your core, but please note that the plank exercise at the end is not recommended for young bodies unless you've done that kind of training before: https://www.youtube.com/watch?v=Jh3HrXHhecl

Dame Darcey Bussell DBE has created a dance fitness programme for schools, called Diverse Dance Mix (DDMIX for Schools): www.ddmixforschools.com. It enables teachers without dance expertise to bring dance fitness into classrooms using a really diverse range of music for all abilities.

BOOKS

Fiction

Gloves Off by Louisa Reid – a YA novel in verse; an exceptionally clever and engaging portrayal of negative body image and how one girl overcomes it in the strongest and most empowering way, through boxing. Boxing and verse: brilliant!

Summer's Dream by Cathy Cassidy – an insight into how some activities, such as ballet, may encourage an unhealthy low weight if you're not careful.

Non-fiction

Healthy for Life: Keeping Fit by Anna Claybourne

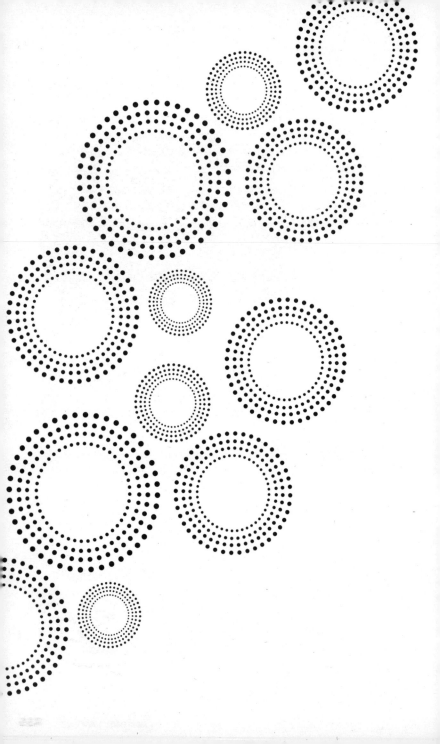

chapter *thirteen*

SLEEP WELL

Scientists used to wonder what sleep was for. Many also look for ways to manage on less of it: after all, think how much more you could get done if you could manage on less sleep!

It turns out that trying to manage with less sleep is a very bad idea. It seems that, even if we still don't know why, sleep is an essential part of making our brain and body work well, be healthy and thrive. Without enough of it, we become vulnerable to a load of problems: bad concentration, low mood, snappiness, mistakes, forgetfulness, inability to learn new things, and even physical illnesses.

Poor sleep even affects appetite and weight: after a bad night, we tend to choose more sugar and fat the next day and be less likely to choose a balanced diet. As you know, there's nothing wrong with any particular food as a choice sometimes but if sleep loss is going to affect our decision-making, that's worth knowing.

Zzz

The trouble is, lying there worrying about the importance of sleep is a sure-fire way not to be able to get to sleep!

I can't promise you'll never have another bad night, because we all have them sometimes and we survive. And even if you have an exam or scary thing the next day, you'll be fine because natural adrenalin will make up for poor sleep for a few nights. But with the advice that follows, I *can* promise to give you more chance of sleeping better. That will mean you're caring for your body better.

HOW DOES SLEEP HELP?

Everything in your body, visible and invisible, will benefit from good sleep: skin, eyes and hair; appetite and weight; your brain's ability to focus; energy to keep your body and brain active; immune system; mood and self-esteem.

During sleep, channels open up in the brain to help brain fluid flow more quickly, to wash away dead cells and waste chemicals. Your brain is doing its own housework as you sleep!

Learning improves, too. Things we tried to learn during the day become consolidated during sleep, with faulty pathways repaired and memories stored, and the next time we try to do those things we succeed better. Sometimes we even solve problems in our sleep, waking up with a flash of inspiration that we just didn't get the day before. Did you know that the chemist Dmitri Mendeleyev is said to have formulated what became the periodic table of elements in his sleep, waking up with the whole idea ready to start writing down? It's interesting to note that this wasn't a random dream: it came after he'd been puzzling over the problem and battling for an answer. If you want to have inspiration in your sleep, you have to work at it!

BODY BOOST

Is your bedroom a relaxing space? Is there anything you could change about it? Tidy it?! Clean sheets are lovely to lie in. Do you need blackout blinds? Maybe an eye mask would be a cheap alternative? Some lovely smells and nicer colours?

Finally, growth hormones are regulated during sleep, so that you grow at the right time and the right amount.

Many of these benefits come more during the later stages of our night-time sleep than the earlier stages, so if we have less sleep overall we risk losing the benefits. So, there's every reason why we should try to get enough good quality sleep. All of us. But how?

First, we need to understand what prevents good sleep...

WHAT STOPS US SLEEPING WELL?

🌱 **Daylight:** human brains are wired to keep us awake by day and asleep at night, and the brain can tell which is which mainly by detecting daylight through a tiny set of cells – the pineal gland – behind the eyes. When the brain thinks it's night-time, it triggers a hormone called melatonin, which keeps you sleepy till morning. Normal electric light doesn't have this effect because it's a different sort of light from daylight, unless it's a special daylight bulb. It still makes sense to use dim light, such as a bedside light, while getting ready for bed, as this is more calming. (Note: some electric lights, including a few bedside lights, are especially designed to mimic daylight. If you have one of these, make sure you don't use it during the evening. Using it when you wake up in the morning *is* a good idea, though.)

🌱 **Light from screens:** the light from almost all screens (except some reading devices) mimics daylight, so using any such device before bed tells your brain to wake up.

🌱 **Strong emotions:** feeling anxious, nervous, sad, angry or excited tend to make it harder to relax. (A reason to keep screens switched off, as they tend to bring alerting messages to our brains, not relaxing ones.) Positive or negative emotions can keep you awake. My most sleepless nights tend to be after I've done a speech and my brain just won't calm down.

🌱 **Depression:** there's a strong link between depressive illnesses and sleep problems. Doctors used to think that depression caused sleep problems, but they now also think that sleep problems can sometimes contribute to depression.

🍂 **A worry:** lying awake worrying is something most of us are familiar with.

🍂 **Being too hot, cold or uncomfortable in any way:** feeling uncomfortable is very distracting.

🍂 **Caffeine:** caffeine is a stimulant, raising heart-rate and keeping us alert. The effects can last many hours. Caffeine is in normal coffee and tea, some fizzy drinks including cola, energy drinks, dark chocolate and a few other things.

🍂 **Strenuous exercise during the evening:** this raises the heart-rate. Exercising earlier in the day can help you sleep, though we don't really know why, but fast exercise during the evening can make it harder to sleep.

🍂 **Too much food:** this makes it uncomfortable to lie down and you may wake up feeling sick or with indigestion. Your digestion slows down a lot when you sleep, so your food can't easily be processed and sits in your stomach.

🍂 **Too little food:** hunger is uncomfortable. We need to be as comfortable as possible for the best sleep.

🍂 **Alcohol:** I know you're not drinking alcohol, but you should know a fact: many people think it helps sleep, but it does the opposite. It may send someone to sleep, but they will wake up a very few hours later feeling terrible.

🍂 **Lack of routine:** although the sleep hormone, melatonin, mainly reacts to darkness, there are other things that help it switch on and off appropriately and one of them is routine. If you always go to bed at different times and do different things in the lead-up to bed-time, you confuse your brain and make it harder to sleep.

→ How can we use this knowledge to sleep better?

Knowing what *stops* us sleeping gives clues about how to sleep better. The important time is the hour or two before bed, when we need to practise 'sleep hygiene'. This involves avoiding things that hinder sleep and choosing things that help sleep.

It's important to realise, though, that not everyone is the same. Be open-minded and try to discover what works best for you.

Here's the best advice, starting about 1.5 hours before we want to feel sleepy:

🍂 **Remove daylight from the room:** ideally, have blackout blinds or curtain lining, so that you really do block the light.

🍂 **Switch off backlit screens** (phones, tablets, computers, TVs): partly because of the light and partly because they are likely to keep you alert.

🍂 **Avoid caffeinated or energy drinks** and heavy or spicy meals.

🍂 **Have a small snack if you're hungry:** maybe milk and a biscuit, or a cheese or turkey sandwich, with lettuce. (Turkey and lettuce are both supposed to help sleep, though the effect will be small.)

🍂 **Be prepared:** get everything ready for the morning, this helps your mind relax and not keep a whole list of things to remember.

🍂 **Have a bath or shower:** but not too hot.

🍂 **Get comfortable:** brush your hair, wash face and hands, wear loose clothing; straighten your sheets and duvet; add extra bedding or a hot water bottle if you're cold.

🍂 **Be mindful:** do gentle stretching or yoga and a breathing exercise. (Search 'belly breathing' or 'relaxation exercise'.)

✦ **Remove your worries:** if you have a worry, write it on a piece of paper, fold it up and put it far from your bed: you can't solve it now, so you're shelving it for tomorrow. Then, give yourself something positive to think about: a dream holiday, what you'd do if you won a million, an adventure you'd love to have.

CREATE A BEDTIME ROUTINE

The brain loves a routine: in other words, the same actions in the same order at about the same time. If we do the same routine before getting into bed, our brain learns that these actions come before bed and sleep and it's more likely to trigger that necessary melatonin.

I believe it's most important to create your *own* routine to suit you, but I've offered an example below. I believe it's really important to start with removing daylight, followed by your choice from all the things listed above. Choose several things and do them in the same order every night for five to ten nights and see what happens.

A sample routine:

1. Eliminate all daylight – close curtains and switch off screens

2. Put work away and get things ready for the morning

3. Have a bath or shower and get into sleepwear

4. Put gentle, quiet music on

5. Spend five minutes on deep breathing and stretching exercises

6. Get into bed and start reading a book.

WHAT ABOUT EBOOK READERS?

If you have an electronic reading device, check whether it is 'backlit' or 'frontlit'. Most computers, tablets and phones are backlit, which makes them easy to read in the dark, but hard to read in sunlight. Frontlighting makes the screen look more like paper and this is commonly how readers are designed.

Backlighting generally uses blue light, having the effect of daylight. Frontlighting has a yellower light and doesn't have as much effect on wakefulness as daylight. But all devices are a bit different and many have settings to adjust the type of light, so it's not always easy to know exactly what you're looking at.

Some devices have 'night-time' settings which claim to allow you to read at night without using the type of light that keeps us awake, but evidence is unclear, mostly suggesting that such settings don't remove the problem, but in some cases may improve it. Future versions may offer better solutions. You can also buy glasses that filter out blue light. Evidence suggests that screen brightness itself hinders sleep, even with a blue light filter. You could do an experiment to see if it makes a difference for you. For one week, read on the normal setting; for one week read on the 'night-time' setting; and for one week read print instead of an ebook. Which is better for sleep? You decide!

BODY BOOST

Read a book in bed. It's such a good way to wind down. Check out the idea of 'readaxation', reading to relax. It works!

If you do want to read on a screen, I won't stop you, as reading has masses of benefits, but try to choose a front-lit screen, one designed for reading books rather than playing games, and use a bedside reading light rather than turning the screen brightness up.

Also make sure that internet connections and notifications are disabled, or you'll find yourself interrupted and alerted and it may be harder to sleep.

Some people find that light from screens doesn't affect their sleep much. They find that the power of being immersed in a great ebook outweighs the possible disadvantage of too much light. Listen to your body and do what works for you.

CAN TELEVISION *HELP* YOU SLEEP?

In theory, televisions in the bedroom are not a good idea. They are bright, noisy and likely to keep you alert. However, watching television can be useful as a winding down activity for someone who has a really big worry or feels very anxious when trying to get to sleep: in those circumstances, watching television might temporarily take their mind off their worries and give them a break.

A big problem, however, is that if you fall asleep with the TV on, you are very likely to wake up again shortly afterwards when a sudden noise happens.

So, while I accept that watching TV for a while to take your mind of worries *could* be a good idea, I strongly recommend not having it in the bedroom and never falling asleep while watching it.

Reading a book would be a much better strategy!

Readaxation - can it help you sleep?

I invented the word **_readaxation_** some years ago to describe the positive effect that burying yourself in an enjoyable book can have on stress. Since stress is one of the things that can keep us awake, reading can certainly help us sleep.

When we're buried in an engaging book which we've chosen, we can forget our worries for a while. It can break our negative thought patterns and calm us down from whatever was agitating us before we went to bed. Being alone with a book is a great feeling because you're not alone: you're with those characters, going through what they're going through, not whatever you're going through. You find yourself thinking of other people, not yourself.

Of course, it's also possible for reading to keep us awake! If the book is gripping enough, we might not want to put it down. I've had that experience. But I think it's a risk worth taking, for the benefits of reading and the very good chance that it will help us sleep.

In fact, some people find they fall asleep too quickly! This illustrates the brain's love of routine: most people had childhood experiences of an adult reading a bedtime story and then putting the light off for sleep. Your brain remembers that as a pattern, so reading in bed can trigger sleep.

How much do we need?

Everyone's different, but on average adults over 20 need seven to eight hours a night and young people from age 12 to 20 need around nine hours or a bit more. If you get much less or much more for many nights in a row, you're likely to notice that you don't feel great and you might experience some of the other negative effects I mentioned (on page 235).

It's fine to have a bit of a catch up on a weekend morning, but it's not a good idea to stay in bed or to sleep for *too* long or to do it on both weekend mornings, as you'll disrupt your sleep patterns. The best way to get more sleep is to go to sleep a bit earlier and get up a bit later.

If you're ill – even with something as minor as a cold – extra sleep can help your body recover. But still be aware that, after more than a day or two, your sleep patterns will be disrupted so keeping to a bedtime and waking routine, even when you're ill, is generally recommended.

If you find that you're falling asleep at inappropriate times, do get yourself checked out by a doctor. It's unlikely to have a medical cause, but it's always worth checking.

Summing up

Sleep is really important for almost every aspect of mental and physical health. It allows our body to regenerate cells, helps us grow properly, and cleans up the debris in our brains, allowing everything to work better. It affects our appetite, weight, skin, growth, concentration, learning, mood and ability to fight disease. You'll look and feel better if you get enough sleep.

Everyone knows the feeling of not being able to sleep, but there are lots of things you can do to have the best sleep possible. Follow the sensible strategies in this book and don't worry if you have the occasional bad night. Use the time to plan the wonderful things you want to do with your brilliant body and mind!

RESOURCES FOR THIS CHAPTER

ONLINE

My website has advice: www.nicolamorgan.com search 'sleep'. Also check out 'readaxation', reading to relax.

The National Sleep Foundation has a useful poster: https://sleepfoundation.org/sites/default/files/sleepcarecenters/2008_Tips_for_Teens_Poster.pdf

The Australian Better Health Channel has lots of detail and is non-patronising: www.betterhealth.vic.gov.au/health/healthyliving/teenagers-and-sleep

The UK NHS site has good info here: www.nhs.uk/live-well/sleep-and-tiredness/sleep-tips-for-teenagers/

Kids Health has this page for adults, but I think you'll find the information useful, too: https://kidshealth.org/en/parents/sleep-problems.html

I like these tips from Dr Craig Capanari, Director of the Yale Pediatric Sleep Center, including some less usual ones: https://drcraigcanapari.com/eight-teen-sleep-tips/

chapter fourteen

YOUR BEST BRILLIANT BODY

Food, exercise and sleep are the three main ways to keep your body strong, fit and ready for the best life, but there are also other things that will affect how you *look*, how you *feel* and how you *feel about how you look*. This all matters to body image and your ability to live the most fulfilled life possible. They all go to make your body brilliant.

Please note that I am not a doctor or medical expert. All the advice in this section is general advice only and should not replace any medical advice. If you are worried about anything, always see a doctor.

MANAGE STRESS

Remember the fourth leg of the four-legged Table of Well-being (see pages 191–2)? It was 'relaxation'. It's really important to control stress levels. Stress is good and necessary when we need to be at peak performance, for an exam, audition, speech, race or competition. But if we feel stressed or anxious too often, the stress chemical, cortisol, builds up. This has negative effects on our bodies and brains.

Stress can come from lots of things and feel different in different people; and it's a word we use to mean lots of varying experiences. In general, however, the body's stress response kicks in when we face *any* challenge or threat or need to perform or react. So, triggers can range from very obvious situations, such as being about to go on stage or do an exam, hearing bad news or having a big worry about someone you love; to things that might seem less obvious, such as a mean comment, being asked a question you don't know the answer to, realising you've done the wrong homework, or just having a sudden worrying thought.

Every 'stressful' thing, whether a thought or an emotion or an event, triggers adrenalin and cortisol to rush around our body, creating the feelings we associate with being stressed or anxious: jitteriness, tension, 'butterflies' in the stomach, nausea and loss of appetite, needing to go to the bathroom a lot, and generally feeling the opposite of relaxed.

→ WHAT HAS STRESS GOT TO DO WITH BODIES?

We think of stress as being in the mind, but it very much affects our body, in lots of ways.

When people are suffering from stress, they often don't look well. They tend to look paler than their usual healthy complexion, and skin may be dry or even grey-looking. They may frown and have tension in the muscles of their face and neck, leading to neck, shoulder or back pain.

Headaches and stomach-aches are common physical symptoms of repeated stress. You might feel sick or dizzy and find it hard to breathe properly. You're more likely to make mistakes, forget things and be snappy with the people around you. Some people might suffer from a feeling of panic or full-scale panic attacks.

Negative stress can affect your immune system, too, making your body more vulnerable to any bug that's going around and meaning that you'll take longer to recover.

WHAT CAN WE DO ABOUT STRESS?

We don't want to eliminate stress from our lives entirely, because stress is necessary to help performance. Besides, it's not harmful if we treat it with respect. To combat the negative possibilities, the key is to build enough opportunities for relaxation into our day. This could be something really small or something bigger and longer. I know you're often really busy, but you're never too busy to take a few minutes out to do a breathing exercise, sit in the sun with your eyes closed or relax your muscles from top to toe. Relaxation can be that easy. If you feel you are too busy, that's the time when you most need to find time to relax.

Here are just a few ideas but you'll have loads more.

BODY BOOST

Make a list of things that relax you and make sure you do one or more every day. But do it consciously, thinking about the wonderful effect it will have. Thinking about the effect makes the effect stronger. You'll find lots of great ideas below.

Ten-minute stress-buster ideas:

♣ Stroke a pet

♣ Walk around the block

♣ Sit in the sun with your eyes closed

♣ Practise a deep breathing relaxation exercise (see the resources)

♣ With your eyes shut, count backwards from 100

♣ Dance to a favourite song

♣ Eat an apple or banana or other fruit, noticing every taste and texture

♣ Make a refreshing glass of water enhanced with any (or all!) of these: ice, a slice of lemon/lime/orange, couple of mint leaves, piece of cucumber.

Things that take longer:

♣ Spend time on a hobby

♣ Go for a run, walk or any other physical activity

♣ Go shopping

♣ Meet a friend for coffee, ice-cream or pizza

♣ Draw a picture, make a poster, write a poem

♣ Bake a cake or biscuits or cook anything you like

♣ Have a long bath

♣ Listen to music with your eyes shut

♣ Go to the cinema, art gallery, museum or concert

♣ Go to a tourist attraction that's near you – maybe one you've never visited.

CHOOSE SOMETHING
TO SUIT *YOUR* STRESS

There are two sorts of stress you might have: you might be feeling generally tense, nervous, over-alert; or you might be preoccupied by a big worry. Both those situations require different approaches.

For the first sort, helpful activities could be: taking a bath, going for a walk or run, mindfulness, listening to music, sitting in the sun. Those activities will all calm you down, lowering your heart rate.

But, if you think about it, if your problem is a big worry, *none of those things will help* because you will probably still have the worry while you're doing them. So, you'd need to choose an activity that occupies lots of your mind: watching an exciting film, reading a gripping book, playing or watching sport, computer gaming, doing a puzzle or anything you have to focus on. All those take up so much of your concentration (often called 'brain bandwidth') that you can't worry at the same time.

BODY BOOST

Walk well. When we feel self-conscious or low, we tend to slouch and walk badly. This makes us feel worse. So, walk tall, keeping your stomach muscles firm; keep your chin up so your neck is well supported; take a deep breath and hold yourself as strongly as possible.

STAY WELL

No one can avoid every bug that's going around and being at school means you're exposed to lots. Every time you get ill, you'll feel lousy and probably miss some work and fun. Prevention is much better than cure, so here's how to have the best chance of avoiding illness.

- **Eat, exercise, sleep and relax:** all four legs of the table will help keep your immune system strong.

- **Treat symptoms as early as possible:** some illnesses are easier to treat than others. With flu and stomach bugs, usually all you can do is treat pain and fever, keep your fluids up and rest, rather than stop the illness altogether. But the very first symptoms of a cold can respond well to the nasal sprays that claim to stop colds; many people also swear by Echinacea at the first signs, though this isn't cheap.

Most illnesses improve with rest and certainly this is not the time to be doing heavy exercise. Use a trusted health website to find out the best strategies for the symptoms you have and always see a doctor if you are at all worried or if you have a high fever, a rash (especially if it doesn't fade when you press a glass on it), or a severe headache with neck pain and visual disturbances. No doctor will think you're silly for checking out anything that's worrying you.

BODY BOOST

Show your body you care about it: treat yourself to a foot soak, long hot bath, moisturiser, new hair-style or product.

❦ **Understand how germs are passed:** one common way to catch something is when our fingers touch the germs and we put our fingers in our mouth or nose or on our food. Some bugs are in the air, usually from coughs or sneezes, so we might breathe in germs when someone has just sneezed, especially if they didn't use a tissue properly.

All of us should be careful and considerate when we have symptoms of a cold, cough or stomach bug. And it's sensible to keep your distance from sneezing, coughing and vomiting people.

People with 'compromised immune systems' (which they will know because their doctors will have told them) are more likely to catch something and become seriously ill. If you know someone like this – someone going through cancer treatment, for example – you should avoid being with them when you have any symptoms.

❦ **Wash hands at the right times:** we don't need to wash our hands at every opportunity, but there are times when we should: before we eat; after going to the toilet; when we've been with someone with an infectious illness; and, ideally, when we've touched something that lots of dirty hands have touched, for example handles, light-switches and taps in public places. (Do keep this in perspective, though: you only need to wash your hands once; if you feel you are washing as carefully as a surgeon or feeling you have to do it with a certain routine, it's possible you are thinking obsessively and you might need help for your anxiety.)

❦ **Fresh air:** germs thrive in warm places with lots of people to pass them around. Opening windows and spending time outdoors is a good way to lower the risks.

 # TEETH

When you consider what a small part of our body our teeth are and how they are often invisible, teeth are a surprisingly important part of our appearance. If you feel that your teeth are misshapen, crowded or discoloured, it can make you feel unconfident and not want to smile. People who don't smile often look less friendly and approachable, so feeling self-conscious about your teeth can really affect your relationships and ability to be outgoing.

So, how can we have the best smile possible?

You will already know about the importance of brushing your teeth properly and not consuming too much sugar. But here are some other things that experts say.

🦷 Dentists recommend NOT brushing your teeth more than two or three times a day, as too much brushing can remove the important top layer of protective enamel. (Some say not more than twice.) Also, don't brush too harshly: use a circular movement rather than a horizontal movement. Ideally use an electric toothbrush. Use only a small amount of toothpaste (a 'pea-sized' amount) and don't rinse, but spit. Rinsing just removes all that good toothpaste that should carry on working after you've brushed. But DO brush twice a day.

🦷 Use fluoride toothpaste unless a doctor or dentist has told you not to.

🦷 If you do consume sugary things, do so with or immediately after a meal.

🦷 Fizzy drinks, such as cola, are especially bad for teeth, partly because the acid in them erodes the tooth's protective enamel and partly because of typically high sugar content, which allows bacteria to grow.

✦ Fruit juice is also acidic and high in sugar.

 "When I was 22, I had veneers put on two front teeth which had quite noticeable white patches because I was going into a career in acting. I asked if there was anything I could 'paint' on my teeth and the dentist laughed and said not yet, so veneers were my only option. I had a brace as a teen but not the train-track type. They're still not straight and I wish I'd pushed to have them straightened more back then. Sometimes in photos I deliberately smile with a closed mouth. I try not to let it bother me too much and it won't stop me laughing!"

Jo

What about flossing?

In 2016 the US government stopped including flossing on its advice guidelines but the American Dental Association points out that this does NOT mean it's not recommended[29]! The government stopped listing it because they wanted to focus on other advice but dentists still recommend using floss or interdental cleaners as a very useful part of your routine. It's often the only way to remove bits of food from between your teeth.

What about mouthwash?

Mouthwash can reach areas of your mouth that normal brushing won't. Some experts[30] are against it, because of the harsh

....

29 https://www.ada.org/en/press-room/news-releases/2016-archive/august/statement-from-the-american-dental-association-about-interdental-cleaners

30 https://askthedentist.com/mouthwash-risks-and-alternatives/

ingredients of some brands. But others[31] say that, as long as it isn't *instead* of good brushing and other hygiene, using mouthwash once a day is fine. Choose one that's approved by the American Dental Association or the UK's Oral Health Foundation.

What about whitening?

Teeth are not naturally gleaming white. And over time they tend to become less white, especially if we drink a lot of tea, coffee or red wine, eat staining foods, such as dark berries or curry, or if we smoke. Although bright white teeth aren't natural, many people nowadays – particularly in the US, some Asian countries and increasingly in other societies, and particularly younger generations – prefer whiter rather than yellower teeth. Many of us will choose whitening toothpastes for this reason.

So, what about toothpaste? Dentists explain[32] that toothpaste can only do 'extrinsic' whitening, which means removing the stains sitting on the outside of your teeth from the food you've just eaten. The stains that actually make teeth look yellow are in the layer beneath that, where toothpaste won't reach. The act of brushing your teeth properly, especially with an electric brush, will have that extrinsic effect whatever toothpaste you use.

 "When my son was a teenager, he stopped smiling because he was embarrassed and self-conscious about his teeth. I didn't know for years and it made me so sad when he told me. He had braces and did start smiling again when they came off and we all kept saying what a lovely smile he had."
Rebecca

....

31 https://www.everydayhealth.com/dental-health/101/specialist/jacobs/need-to-use-mouthwash.aspx

32 https://askthedentist.com/best-whitening-toothpaste/

What about the other whitening methods? In the UK, teeth whitening is the fastest-growing cosmetic procedure. In the US, artificially bright white teeth are very common and some treatments that are available over the counter are not available in the UK, because there are different safety rules. And the advice is clear: talk to your dentist before considering anything. Your dentist will be able to say what's appropriate for you and will be able to ensure that whatever you choose is safe.

I investigated whether there was any different advice for teenagers compared to adults and found a lot of warnings to say either that there wasn't enough research and testing to be sure of safety or that there are more risks for young people. Some advice strongly recommends waiting till you're over 16 and some places won't treat teenagers. You certainly need to be more careful than adults and even adults are advised always to seek a dentist's opinion first. Some kits that you can buy cause damage if wrongly used and all whitening treatment should be carried out or supervised by a qualified dentist.

One day, scientists may develop a safer method, but meanwhile it will be much better to clean your teeth well and avoid the drinks and foods that stain.

If you have any worries about staining on your teeth, for example perhaps you have one tooth that's darker, do ask your dentist. They understand the importance of having teeth that we can be confident about and they will listen carefully and help if they can. There are procedures, such as veneers, that only a dentist can offer.

What about chewing gum?

Chewing gum – as long as it's sugar-free – can help keep your mouth and teeth healthy. It increases saliva flow to neutralise the acid from food or drink we've just eaten and remove food particles, including dislodging bits of food between teeth.

Evidence suggests that the artificial sweetener, xylitol, is effective in reducing certain bacteria that cause cavities, so choose a sugar-free variety that contains this sweetener.

Dentists point out that chewing gum can't replace good cleaning practices but it can be a useful extra. It's also important to note that if you have jaw pain, you usually shouldn't chew gum but check with a dentist first.

Please, whatever you do, dispose of your gum properly!

What about straightening?

Teenagers and teeth-straightening have been partners for a long time. And sometimes adults have it done, too. It's never exactly pleasant, but most people are pleased with the results. Many teenagers don't mind about the appearance aspect of wearing braces – perhaps because it's so common – but others will find it more difficult. There's some temporary pain each time the braces are tightened, and eating some foods is somewhat complicated and unattractive, but the procedure is safe. Newer techniques are gentler and can be more discreet – or more fun and colourful if that's what you prefer. Depending on where you live, there may be a cost, especially if it's purely cosmetic rather than medical or functional.

SKIN

Your skin needs varied foods with all the nutrients, water and fresh air. It also likes to be clean, but doesn't need to be too clean as you'll wash away all the natural oils. Some people have oilier and others have drier skin, and the differences are particularly noticeable on facial skin. Some people have a 'combination' skin, an oily T-shaped zone covering forehead, nose and chin, and a drier area elsewhere. Oily skin is ultimately good because it will be less prone to flaking and when you're older you'll be the envy of all your friends because oilier skin remains youthful-looking for longer. But oily skin is often more prone to spots and acne, particularly when you're young.

Acne

When I was young, people knew very little about the causes of acne. We were told that chocolate or greasy food caused it, or lack of hygiene, or stress. Now, we know a bit more, though not everything. Many pieces of research into causes and treatments are performed on tiny numbers of people, which make them really not meaningful, so be cautious about advice that doesn't seem to be from a reputable source, particularly if the article or website is trying to sell a product.

What do we now know about causes? The main cause is the hormone, androgen, which increases during puberty in both boys and girls, which is why both boys and girls get acne. And it's usually a bigger problem for teenagers than adults, typically disappearing in adulthood. When androgen levels rise, glands under the skin produce more oil. When the pores become full of oil, the cells nearby can break and bacteria get in. The bacteria cause a tiny infection which becomes a pimple or spot. And those spots can be in many places, not just on the face but often on the back, for example, and less commonly elsewhere. These spots often become inflamed – that's the redness you see around them – and treatment aims to reduce that inflammation.

Some people suffer very severe acne and others get away with the occasional spot or break out. Those differences are partly genetic, partly relating to the oiliness of skin, and partly dependent on your hormone levels and how your body reacts to them. Research also suggests a link with the type of 'friendly bacteria' you have on your skin.

Does food make a difference?

It may do but the research is quite unclear. The problem is that the effects of foods are very complicated. Each food contains many components and everyone's body is different, with varying hormone levels and different chemical processes. Also, it's very difficult to create a study that examines the effects of any particular food because most people are eating lots of different things and it can be impossible to work out which one is having an effect.

But, looking at recent research[33], foods that *may possibly* make acne worse at least in some people include: refined sugars (processed sugars, rather than sugar found naturally in fruit, for example), milk, fast foods high in fats, chocolate and whey protein. But everyone's reaction will be different, as we are not all sensitive to the same things. Experts tend to say that foods don't cause acne, though some may make it worse.

If you suspect that your acne is worse after eating certain things, ask your doctor to help you do a special elimination experiment. Or, if your suspect food is something simple to avoid, try avoiding it for two weeks and note down how your acne is each day. (Do not try radically restricting your food without medical advice, or you may well miss vital nutrients.)

Some foods may help. Again, research has not brought definite conclusions, but any of these might be worth a try (and they are great foods anyway): foods rich in vitamins A, D, E and zinc, such as milk, eggs, oily fish, fortified cereals, green leafy veg, whole grains;

33 https://www.healthline.com/nutrition/foods-that-cause-acne#section1 (Note that although the heading is about causes of acne, the article is careful *not to say that any of these are causes!*)

green tea; turmeric. Some people recommend probiotics (in 'live' yogurt). A diet rich in fresh, raw fruit and veg, as well as the oils you find in olives, avocadoes and oily fish, such as mackerel, has also been recommended. In fact, the best food-related thing you can do for acne is eat a really great diet, filled with fresh fruits and veg, and following all the advice in chapter eleven.

One useful thing you can do if you have acne is to keep a diary, recording days when it was better or worse. That way, you might see a pattern, and that might allow you to try to modify your habits to help your acne. On the other hand, be careful about leaping to conclusions: if you think it is a particular thing, you'll need to test that out quite a bit before you can feel sure.

Make-up

It will probably be tempting to use make-up to cover acne on your face. It's generally better not to, because it tends to clog the pores even more and allow more harmful bacteria onto your face. But I completely understand if you sometimes want to do this. If so, choose products that are designed for acne-prone skin. These will usually be oil-free, may be described as 'non-comedogenic' (meaning they shouldn't cause spots) and sometimes include anti-inflammatory ingredients. You certainly don't want something that might irritate your skin. Try it on a small area first.

Most people with acne find it distressing and preoccupying, just at a time in your life when you're probably particularly self-conscious and when people can be cruel to you. It can contribute to anxiety and depression, too. It's important to get the most up-to-date advice and help and also to get the advice early, rather than waiting for the acne to become worse. Your doctor is the best place to start. Once you've done that, there's also great advice online in websites especially for teenagers.

Clean skin

Keeping your skin clean is a good idea for everyone and there are many products on the market. But don't overdo the face-washing, as you will wash away all the natural oils and friendly bacteria that help keep your skin healthy. And don't feel you have to spend lots of money: you can even make your own facial cleansers! I put the phrase 'home-made facial wash' into a search engine and (after ignoring the adverts) quickly came up with several websites where people shared their recipes. I didn't find any with weird or dangerous substances, but if you've got any doubts about the genuine healthiness of what you're looking at, ask a sensible adult! Even products that sound super-healthy and natural, such as lemon juice, can be quite strong on delicate facial skin.

> *"There's nothing wrong with spending money on face creams and things like that: if pampering makes you feel happy then do it."*
> **Charlie, 13**

Skin can occasionally react unexpectedly so test anything by putting a bit in the inside of your wrist for half an hour. If there's any redness, don't put it on your face.

There are some ethnic differences in good skin care regimes[34], as

34 https://int.eucerin.com/about-skin/basic-skin-knowledge/skin-ethnics

well as individual differences, so always follow the advice for your skin type.

Sun protection

One of the most important ways to care for your skin, especially if you're pale, is to protect it from the sun and wind. Wear sun-cream in the summer and on any sunny day if you're outside. And, ideally, use daily moisturiser with an SPF factor of at least 30.

People with all skin colours need to protect themselves from sun damage, but the lighter your skin the more vulnerable you are.

Away from your face

The rest of our body needs attention, too! Skin is our body's largest organ and it's usually only when we damage it that we see how important it is. Luckily, it's pretty easy to look after: we need to keep it clean enough, including in all the cracks and wrinkles; protect it from becoming too dry (by drinking enough water; occasionally gently exfoliating; and moisturising if we want to or our skin feels tight and dry); and look out for any problems, whether rashes, bumps, moles that grow or bleed, or anything we think looks not right and that a doctor should take a look at. Most things turn out to be nothing, but it's never wrong to check.

There are lots of skin conditions, most of which can be fairly simply treated with a cream or other medication from your doctor. Everything responds better if it's caught early, so do get an appointment. Skin conditions can be anything from one strange mark that doesn't go away to rashes covering larger areas. Almost all of them will be nothing serious and many will either disappear or be treatable. But they can also be a sign of something serious which needs to be treated early.

Two important examples of things you should not ignore are:

- ✦ A mole or other raised mark that grows, changes in appearance and/or bleeds – many of these are harmless, but occasionally (more often in adults) they are an early sign of something more serious. It's not an emergency but you should not delay seeing your doctor.

- ✦ A rash that doesn't disappear when you press a glass onto it, if you are feeling ill, with a fever, or feeling as if you have flu with muscle aches, sore throat or headache. You should get urgent medical attention in case these are signs of a type of meningitis. This is a hospital emergency.

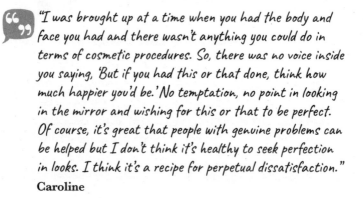

"I was brought up at a time when you had the body and face you had and there wasn't anything you could do in terms of cosmetic procedures. So, there was no voice inside you saying, 'But if you had this or that done, think how much happier you'd be.' No temptation, no point in looking in the mirror and wishing for this or that to be perfect. Of course, it's great that people with genuine problems can be helped but I don't think it's healthy to seek perfection in looks. I think it's a recipe for perpetual dissatisfaction."
Caroline

Eczema (also known as dermatitis)

This can affect almost any part of the body and can be extremely itchy and may not be nice to look at. You might scratch so much that the skin breaks and then it can become infected. It's more common in children and young people than adults, though anyone can get it.

You might have just one or two recurring patches or it might cover large areas of your body. The skin is dry but may also be red, cracked and inflamed, so treatment and prevention involve trying not to let the affected areas dry out, and avoiding certain chemicals and trigger factors, which will vary from person to person. Soap and many cleaning products tend to dry our skin so you'll be given 'emollient' products to use instead, but it's incredibly difficult to avoid soap and similar products.

If you have eczema, you may have heard doctors say that you are 'atopic'. This means that you have a tendency to have 'allergic' conditions, such as eczema, asthma, rhinitis, hay fever. Your immune system seems to be extra sensitive to various things in the environment or food. Everyone's 'atopy' will be a bit different, but part of what your doctor will try to help you do is find out which things make your eczema worse or better.

You'll usually be offered a cream to use and if this doesn't work there are others to try so don't be disappointed if the first one doesn't work.

As well as seeing your doctor, you might research online. Focus on the official organisations run by your country's health service or the main charities that work in whatever condition you have.

HAIRCARE

Like skin, healthy hair needs the right foods and good care. You might have heard that hair is dead, but actually the roots beneath the skin are very much alive and hair is the fastest-growing tissue in the body. Everyone's hair is different and we inherit a lot of its features from our biological parents.

Ethnicity makes a difference to hair texture and also to how to care for it. By now, you've probably discovered the best places to get advice for your type of hair and that's really important. For example, some people will need to oil their hair regularly, whereas others won't. If you're following YouTubers, take advice from one with the same ethnic background as you.

 "My hair is hard to keep healthy so I spend time and money on this, not to make it look good but to be healthy."
Daisy, 14

Hair health

At your age, things that will make the most difference to your hair are:

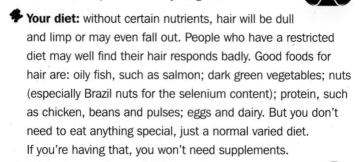

🍀 **Your physical health:** hair tends to react to illness, whether a simple cold or anything else.

🍀 **Your diet:** without certain nutrients, hair will be dull and limp or may even fall out. People who have a restricted diet may well find their hair responds badly. Good foods for hair are: oily fish, such as salmon; dark green vegetables; nuts (especially Brazil nuts for the selenium content); protein, such as chicken, beans and pulses; eggs and dairy. But you don't need to eat anything special, just a normal varied diet. If you're having that, you won't need supplements.

🍀 **The weather or swimming:** very cold weather tends to make our hair drier and brittle, and swimming can strip the oils away, too. Try a rich conditioner to nourish your hair and there are various hair oils on the market for occasional or regular use. Always choose one that's right for your hair type.

🌿 **Too much styling:** using heat to curl or straighten, or even using a hair-dryer on a very high heat setting for too long, dries out your hair. Too much heat risks damaging hair. Limit how much you use these tools.

🌿 **Too many products:** the products can build up and make your hair feel lank, sticky or heavy. Make sure you wash and rinse your hair thoroughly.

> *"Growing up in India, I had body image problems through my teens. I was too thin for starters. I didn't play sports or dance, so was always clumsy. My clothes weren't nice and that added to the embarrassment. I thought I looked weird and peers and relatives made fun of how thin I was. Also, I had long hair and I wasn't allowed to cut or style it."*
> **Selvi**

My simple haircare advice is:

🌿 Follow advice from people who understand your hair type, but be cautious of people trying to sell you something, especially something expensive.

🌿 Eat well.

🌿 Keep your hair clean (but don't wash more than necessary), brush it regularly and don't spend more than you can afford on products. You might sometimes use egg white as a mask for a few minutes before a shower; or put a bit of olive oil on the ends if they're dry.

Hair-pulling

Compulsive hair-pulling is something that an estimated 1–2 per cent of people do, more often females. It's called trichotillomania and is an impulse-control disorder: the person doesn't really want to do it, but they can't seem to resist – a bit like nail-biting but less common. It's usually associated with anxiety and treatment involves dealing with that anxiety and finding alternative and positive strategies.

The reason it comes into a book on body image is that if your hair-pulling leads to bald patches (or if you pull out your eyelashes) then it's going to create something about your appearance that may make you feel more anxious and negative. Do see a doctor so you can get the best help. Trying to resist the temptation yourself isn't usually the answer as it can make the urge stronger.

> *"How my hair is each day makes a major difference to how I think I look and how I feel. Sometimes I don't even want to go to school if it looks terrible."*
> **Jessica, 17**

FINGERNAILS AND TOENAILS

Whether it's the effects of sport or swimming, helping your parents with household or garden chores, or the fact that you bite your nails and just can't stop, the ends of fingers can take a battering.

But, although it can be difficult, it does *not* need to be expensive. You don't need to go for manicures. In fact, doing too much to your nails, and especially using acrylic nails or wearing nail polish all the time, can weaken them – though doing this occasionally is no problem.

Our overall health makes a difference and sometimes doctors look at nails to detect signs of illness or vitamin deficiency. So, the first thing for great nails is a great diet, where you get all the nutrients you need from food.

Moisturise your hands if they feel dry, and pay special attention to the cuticles (the skin at the bottom edge and sides of the nail). Be really careful not to push the cuticles too hard – you can leave them where they are as long as you moisturise them.

Trim nails to the length that feels right for you and allows you to do what you need to do, whatever that is. Over-long nails break easily and are not useful for loads of activities!

All that care applies to toenails, although toenails should be cut really carefully and only straight across, to avoid the edge of the nail growing into the skin. One extra thing to look out for with toenails is fungal infections. (You can get this on fingernails, too, but that's much less common.) If a nail goes thick and yellow, it's probably a fungal infection. It could clear up with special cream or a doctor might prescribe tablets. But it's unlikely to go away by itself and could spread, so do see a doctor. Any painful red area on a toe or finger could be another kind of infection so if it persists or gets worse, get it looked at.

Nail-biting

You're either a nail-biter or you're not; if you are it's very difficult to stop. You'll often not even know you're doing it and it might not be the nail, but the cuticles or edges of your fingers. It's estimated that about half of people in the US are nail-biters. It's a big deal for people who have it and it even has a name: onychophagia.

It's a type of compulsive disorder and seems to be connected to anxiety or mood disorders, though lots of people who do it don't have other diagnoses of mental health problems. People often notice that they'll do it more when they are worried or stressed and it seems to be a kind of coping mechanism, though it's not a positive one.

How can you stop?

Telling the nail-biter to stop tends not to work. It usually means that as soon as they're in private they'll do it more. It's an urge that's very hard to resist if that's the habit their brain has formed.

There are nasty-tasting substances you can buy to put on your fingers, but these are not usually effective. They could be worth trying, though, as they aren't expensive and they work for some people. A simple solution, such as wearing gloves, can help you break the habit. I have not read any research about the use of hypnotherapy for this but I imagine it could well be effective for some people. And CBT, which I've talked about before, can also help by reducing anxiety.

Because it's a habit, the best way to tackle it is to disrupt the 'habit loop' with a different action. So, each time you're tempted to put your finger in your mouth, do something else. The 'something else' has to be something pleasant or rewarding – a really good option is to drink a couple of sips of water. You have to do the same each time, so as to create a new habit.

Of course, you might not have water with you and you might not notice you're about to bite your nails. But it's not as hard as you might think, as long as you don't expect instant results. The key is to distract yourself with a different and more positive action. Don't use punishment: use reward.

Give yourself a break from work; sniff a gorgeous smell; take ten deep breaths; look out of the window.

Don't worry if you sometimes find you bite your nails without noticing: just praise yourself each time you do manage to replace nail-biting with something good.

Personal Hygiene ←

Keeping ourselves clean is important for lots of reasons. There's the health angle: being dirty can lead to skin infections or fungal infections (though even very clean people can get these) and in some cases can make us more likely to catch illnesses, particularly if our hands are dirty and we put them in our mouth.

Being dirty can also make us smell unattractive and, like it or not, humans are very sensitive to smell – and some more than others. One of the distressing things about being homeless is how hard it is to keep clean and fresh-smelling. This affects people's confidence, self-respect and even ability to make friends and have relationships.

Having a daily shower, washing our hair when it looks and feels as though it needs it, keeping our hands clean and brushing our teeth twice a day – that's all we usually need to keep ourselves clean enough and show respect for our bodies.

Some people sweat more than usual. This is called hyperhidrosis. It can affect the armpits, palms of hands and soles of feet, and sometimes other areas, such as the groin. Although there's usually no underlying medical reason, it's an upsetting problem to have, but there are various treatments that can work really well, some temporary and some permanent. Your doctor can help.

Some people have a different problem with sweat: body odour. Everyone has body odour sometimes, but for some people it's more difficult to control. Sometimes you know you've got it and this can make you feel unconfident, especially when you have to be near people. Sometimes you've done everything right in terms of washing and using anti-perspirant, but you still might sweat more than other people. But do remember that it is entirely normal to sweat and that the sweat in some areas of our body normally smells more. During a school day it's highly likely that you'll sweat.

What can you do about this?

🐾 Wash every morning and, if you want, when you come home from school. Try an anti-bacterial soap, to deal with the bacteria that cause the smell. Make sure you dry yourself properly.

🐾 Apply a good anti-perspirant deodorant. 'Anti-perspirant' and 'deodorant' are two different things: the first contains chemicals to reduce sweating and the deodorant part just introduces a nice smell. The anti-perspirant is the important bit.

🐾 If a normal anti-perspirant isn't working for you, look for a 'high-strength' one. These didn't exist over the counter when I was your age, but now they are easy to find – though more expensive than normal ones. They work really well, but watch out for redness and soreness as some of them are very strong; it might take time to find the one the suits you best. Don't apply more often than the instructions say and don't apply to broken skin.

🐾 Wear a clean shirt or top every day and, of course, clean underwear.

If you really think you sweat more than most people, it's always a good idea to see a doctor. There may be a particular solution, including some CBT if it seems that your sweating could be related to stress or to worrying about sweating.

BLUSHING

Most people will know the feeling of blushing: it *feels* so ridiculous, because it's always when people are looking at you and the more you notice that you're blushing the more you're likely to blush. As I say, most people have experienced this, but some people experience it a lot. There'll be no physical or medical reason: it's purely a reaction to feeling self-conscious. It's a faulty stress response – faulty because it doesn't actually do any good. (It doesn't do any harm, either.)

What to do about it? The best thing is try to ignore it, but that's easier said than done. Certainly, the more you think about trying not to blush, the more you're likely to blush. If this starts happening, allow the thought to go in and out of your head: 'Oh, right, I'm blushing – never mind: I'll focus on the face of the person I'm talking to.' The key is to avoid thinking 'I mustn't think about blushing' because as soon as we tell ourselves not to think about something, that's exactly what we think about! Instead, focus on thinking about the face in front of you or anything else at all.

If blushing is a major problem for you, see what your doctor can recommend. Hypnotherapy can work very well for things like this and you don't need to see a doctor first – though you will have to pay.

Blemishes and cosmetic surgery

In chapter eight, I discussed visible differences, where people may have major scarring from accidents or disfigurement from illness or a condition they were born with. As you know, there are often ways that surgery can improve appearance if the person wishes. On the other hand, in chapter three, I expressed a negative opinion of people using surgery to make their bodies more perfect than they are. So, there are two different situations, one where cosmetic surgery can help and one where it's likely to be an expensive route to continued dissatisfaction.

> *"I think the idea of plastic surgery is awful and it can go wrong."*
> **Bella 15**

But what if you have something about your body which isn't a major visible difference, but which is still really distressing you, a birthmark or lump or scar, for example? Maybe it's not even something people see while you're dressed, but it makes you hate taking your clothes off when people are looking? Maybe it's something about which other people would say, 'Oh, don't be silly – that's nothing!' But it's still affecting you. It looks small to others but to you it's big.

Is it OK to ask about cosmetic surgery for this? Of course, it is! It's always OK to ask your doctor about anything that's worrying you. It's all very well for me to say you're supposed to love and respect your brilliant body, but maybe there really is just this one thing that's holding you back. And maybe it would be simple to get rid of it. Maybe it's something that isn't 'supposed' to be there and you wish it wasn't.

 "I think that people having cosmetic surgery just to change your shape is wrong. It isn't natural to 'edit' your body like that."
Harris, 14

From your doctor, you *might* discover that it's not possible to remove it or that it will be too expensive or risky. On the other hand, it might be simple and cheaper than you fear.

So, yes, it's *always* fine to ask about anything that's worrying you. Say how you feel and don't feel embarrassed. If you think your doctor isn't listening or understanding, you can ask to see someone else. They are experts, though, and if they say it's risky or not advisable, it's important to listen. In that case, a talking therapy, such as CBT, could be a good idea.

 "If people have cosmetic surgery to make themselves look better, I think they are representing themselves in a negative way. People should be independent and not afraid of who they are."
Siedd, 13

It's very important to get expert advice from someone who doesn't benefit financially from your surgery. Procedures should be performed by properly qualified people (look for letters after their names, not fancy websites) and you should be screened for mental health conditions, particularly BDD. In chapter seven, I pointed out that patients with severe BDD typically aren't helped by surgery because the problem is distorted thinking and surgery doesn't tackle that.

However, if you want a procedure to enhance or diminish a perfectly brilliant part of your body just because it doesn't live up to some artificial ideals, I hope you choose not to. I hope you come to realise that your body is brilliant without moving fat from one place to the next or inserting something artificial into it. Be yourself: be brilliant!

 "Plastic surgery is common among Kpop artists who fix minor blemishes on their face so they all look the same."

Daisy, 14

Summing up

As well as the core areas of food, exercise and sleep, there are other ways we should show respect for our brilliant bodies: managing stress, keeping well, looking after our teeth, skin, hair and nails, all help make us feel and look great. We won't always feel great and we won't always look our best but we owe it to ourselves to care for our brilliant bodies the best we can. Our choices make a difference.

RESOURCES FOR
THIS CHAPTER

STRESS:

Two of my books have lots of tips about stress management: *The Teenage Guide to Stress* and *Positively Teenage*.

TEETH:

Whitening – advice from the US: www.netdoctor.co.uk/beauty/dental/a29127/teeth-whitening-dentist-recommendation/

And the UK: www.nhs.uk/live-well/healthy-body/teeth-whitening/

Great advice here: www.nhs.uk/live-well/healthy-body/how-to-keep-your-teeth-clean/

Mouthwash pros and cons: www.everydayhealth.com/dental-health/to-mouthwash-or-not-to-mouthwash.aspx

SKIN:

Acne advice: www.webmd.com/skin-problems-and-treatments/acne/features/avoiding-the-angst-of-acne-at-any-age#1 and www.aad.org/public/diseases/acne-and-rosacea/teenage-acne

Acne causes: www.mayoclinic.org/diseases-conditions/acne/symptoms-causes/syc-20368047

Ethnic differences in skin texture: https://int.eucerin.com/about-skin/basic-skin-knowledge/skin-ethnics

HAIR:

From Teen Help.com: www.teenhelp.com/skin-care-grooming/hair-care/

From Hair Scientists on nutrition and hair: www.hairscientists.org/hair-and-scalp-conditions/nutrition-and-hair-health

Haircare for boys: www.quora.com/What-are-some-of-the-hair-care-tips-for-teenage-boys

NAILS:

Nail health: www.everydayhealth.com/skin-and-beauty-pictures/ways-to-keep-your-nails-healthy.aspx

Nail-biting: www.psychologytoday.com/us/conditions/onychophagia-nail-biting

COSMETIC PROCEDURES:

If you are thinking about or wanting cosmetic surgery, see Cosmetics Support: http://www.cosmeticsupport.com/

Lip-filler advice: www.teenvogue.com/story/lip-injections-what-to-expect

South Korea plastic surgery – 'Escape the corset': www.nytimes.com/2018/11/23/business/south-korea-makeup-plastic-surgery-free-the-corset.html

And: www.theguardian.com/world/2018/oct/26/escape-the-corset-south-korean-women-rebel-against-strict-beauty-standards

chapter fifteen

SELF-EXPRESSION AND SELF-RESPECT

You've given your body great food, exercised it to make it strong, worked on getting the best sleep you can, and made sure you moderate stress with relaxation – all the legs of my table of well-being. But alongside that, there are some other things you could do to feel as confident as possible in your brilliant body.

DRESS FOR YOU

Sometimes we have to dress how other people tell us. At your age, you'll get that more than I do, but adults also have to follow dress-code rules, whether it's a work-place dress-code or actual uniform, or having to dress in a certain way for a social function. And, of course, there are different cultural rules. But there are three things that can make this particularly difficult for your age: first, you're changing physically and it can take time to work out what suits you best. Second, the people around you may be judging you very openly, more than most adults would have to face. Thirdly, most school uniform is not flattering!

I won't encourage you to push school uniform boundaries: the rules and the reasons for them are between you and your school. But I do want to encourage you to experiment with style at times when you can. Don't be afraid to make mistakes – they'll soon be forgotten! (Or you can laugh about them one day.)

> *"Uniform can either help or hinder a person's self-confidence and how they think about how they look. On the one hand, if everyone looks the same it's easier to fit in and not be judged. On the other hand, it can hinder self-confidence because it doesn't give you the chance to express yourself in a way that suits you."*
> **David, 14**

It's entirely up to you whether you dress to impress or shock or fit in, whether you want to be bold and bright, dark and gloomy, heavily made-up or not. If you want to try something, go for it. Browse charity shops, learn to sew, upcycle, adapt, get creative.

You'll find websites that advise about the so-called 'rules' of whether vertical or horizontal stripes or floral patterns or various colours might suit your shape or height or colouring better than others, but the best rule is: if you like it on you, wear it. Some of those 'rules' don't work as well as you might think! And they're exactly the sort of rule that's perfect for breaking, in my opinion.

When you change how you express yourself, don't be surprised if you get some comments that might make you feel more self-conscious. Often, people react with surprise just because it's different from what you usually look like. It doesn't necessarily mean they don't like it, even if their reaction is laughter. Persevere. It's up to you when you change your style, not anyone else.

If you want to, ask a friend what they think. Tell them you really want to know. Ideally do this at a time when you could change outfit: you don't want to ask at the start of an evening out and then feel uncomfortable for hours. And be aware that you may be putting your friend in a difficult situation, so it's important that if they give you an honest but negative opinion, you respect them for that and don't make them feel bad. Be clear about what you want to know and if you can't face a negative opinion, don't ask.

On the other hand, it's only one person's opinion. Others might disagree. The most important opinion is your own. Once you get a reputation for dressing a bit differently or surprisingly, people will soon start to respect you.

Often when I visit schools, there'll be a couple of students in each year who I'll identify as the ones who dare to be a bit different in some way, whether in hair or clothes or make-up. I have massive respect for those people: they are the person I never dared to be.

BODY BOOST

Find your style and play with it. Often, we get stuck with one shape of clothing when there are lots we haven't tried. Just changing the neck line or style of a top or even the colour you wear can make a big difference to how you feel about your body. Get a friend to help you. Go shopping, trying things on without any pressure to buy.

→ MAKE-UP AND MAKING THE MOST OF OURSELVES

None of you need make-up advice from me! You've got your favourite vloggers and YouTubers to give you everything you need to know. It's entirely your choice whether you go fresh-faced or use a bit of make-up, as long as you're doing it for yourself.

Some people might criticise me for being positive about make-up. What's good about hiding your natural face, they might ask? But we humans have painted faces and bodies for many thousands of years, to enhance whatever we want to enhance, to look our best when we want to, to play with appearance in creative ways. I'm not saying it's good or bad: I'm saying do it if you want to and if it makes you feel better. However, see the next words of caution!

 "I spend money and time on beauty products because it makes me feel good. Lots of my friends do it too but we're not obsessed with it."
Ninnah, 14

I'd strongly urge you not to spend too much – cheaper brands can be just as effective. I'd also recommend finding a routine that doesn't take too long. It's certainly true that a lot of techniques and products are very time-consuming and I'm pretty sure you've got other things to spend your time on. But it's your choice: do it for yourself. If it's genuinely making you feel better and fit into a group that's important to you, I don't criticise you for that.

Wearing make-up can give you confidence and that's a good thing. It can help you feel your best. And it can be a great social and bonding activity with your friends as you get ready for a party. It can allow you to express yourself, too, whatever your gender and sexuality. You can experiment. And it washes off!

 "I think when girls put make-up on they are saying they don't like their natural face."

Sasha, 14

POSTURE - WALK TALL

When we feel bad, physically or mentally, we tend to slouch. We might fold our arms, hunching over. And the other side of the coin is also true: when we don't walk tall, we don't *feel* great. People even use the phrase 'walk tall' as a metaphor for facing the world proudly and strongly.

If you consciously walk or stand in a strong, tall, proud way, holding your head high – literally and metaphorically – you'll feel better and stronger, instantly. Try it!

There are three main tricks and they apply whether you're standing, walking or sitting:

1. Imagine there's a string attached to the top of your head, pulling you up. You're trying to be as tall as possible, to stretch your spine and neck. And you're trying not to lean forward.

2. Learn to 'engage your core'. Our core muscles are the muscles that support our abdomen and spine. You'll be using them all the time you're walking, sitting or standing, but we all benefit from making sure we really work these muscles well, to prevent injury. And most people don't use their core properly at all. Videos are the best way to get the hang of this, unless you're lucky enough to know a fitness or pilates trainer, so search online for one that you like.

3. Relax your shoulders down and back. So many of us tend to hold tension in our shoulders and necks and this isn't a good way to stand, sit or walk.

DON'T POLLUTE YOUR BODY

Tobacco, alcohol and other drugs do your brilliant body no favours. They all have different effects and research strongly suggests that most – and perhaps all – have stronger and worse effects on young people than on most older adults. All these substances are potentially addictive – some more than others – but addiction is not the only risk. For details about the various harmful effects of any drug, including tobacco and alcohol, check out the resources at the end of the chapter.

Of course, some are illegal – or there are age restrictions for others – but legality is not the only issue. There are also substances – such as alcohol or 'legal highs' – which can also do a great deal of harm, particularly to young brains. Often, they're only legal because scientists haven't had a chance to test them. Don't risk being a guinea pig!

Note as well that some countries have very harsh punishments for people carrying or using some substances that might be legal in your country.

To respect your body and brain and help them be as brilliant as possible, avoid these toxins.

CONSENT – YOUR BODY, YOUR CHOICE

No one should do things to your body (or images of your body) that you don't consent to. And saying yes because you've been forced to, physically or emotionally, doesn't count as consent.

When we talk about consent, we usually mean this in the context of sexual activity. Each country has different laws about this, including the 'age of consent', the age at which someone may legally have sexual activity. *Both* partners must be the required age.

The law

It's very important to know what your country's laws says about sexual consent. Whether you're wanting your partner to do something or they're wanting you to do something, it is wrong (and usually illegal) to do something that the other person doesn't want or to try to persuade or force them to want it. No means no.

If you are in a sexual relationship, make sure you are protected by appropriate contraception, not just to avoid unwanted pregnancy but also to protect you against disease. Again, different countries have different laws and different options for young people in sexual relationships, all of which you'll be able to find online. Be informed, be in control, be safe.

Your right to decide

But consent isn't just about sex. It's also about your right to decide who touches your body. Of course, someone might touch you accidentally and sometimes there are activities that require you to hold hands with someone or touch them in some other way. Holding hands in a game can make some people feel uncomfortable, but I think most people would agree that this isn't something we can usually object to, unless there's a particular reason for our discomfort with that person, in which case we certainly should not be forced to do it.

Some people are more 'tactile' than others: they are more comfortable touching and being touched and may not really think about it. Some of your friends might hug each other or use all sorts of other physical signs of friendship. If you're uncomfortable about this, you can just not join in these activities. If they are genuine friends, they won't mind at all. You might want to explain that it makes you feel uncomfortable, but that you still love being with them and talking.

Medical consent

There's also medical consent. Different countries and states have different laws about the age at which a young person can say yes to a medical procedure, rather than their parent being consulted, and different ages at which young people can be assured of confidentiality. Check what the age for medical consent is where you live.

Changing at school

At school, you might have to get undressed in front of other people and you might not like this. (I don't think many people like it much, to be honest.) Schools ought to treat this situation sensitively and they have a duty to treat all students with dignity, be sensitive to their needs and respect cultural or religious views. If you believe that how you're required to get undressed doesn't follow these guidelines or you feel really uncomfortable, discuss it with a trusted teacher. I bet you'll find you're not the only person who feels uncomfortable.

Photos and consent

Finally, there's one form of consent that's really hard to enforce and frequently ignored: consent for photos of you to be taken and shared. First, let me emphasise that sharing or possessing any

photos of a person under the age of 18 in any kind of sexual pose – including nude or exposing any part of genitalia – is against the law in many countries.

This is so important and also such a big problem for many young people, that I want to say something more. It has become common for young people, even as young as ten, to feel pressured to send a naked or partially naked picture of themselves. In relationships, some girls (and also sometimes boys) feel strongly pressured to do this, with their boy- or girlfriend making all sorts of threats if they don't.

I cannot over-emphasise how sad and unacceptable this is. If you send a picture of yourself or part of your body, you will be highly likely to wish you hadn't. Someone who likes and respects you would not ask you to do this and you should not feel you have to obey. Yes, it's against the law but, more importantly, it's risky for the person sending the picture and cruel, hateful and deeply disrespectful behaviour by the person exerting the pressure. It is your body and no one should make you do anything that puts you at risk.

 "I think it's wrong to take or publicly post a photo of someone without their consent unless the person obviously has a certain confidence level and the person taking the photo knows them well. But otherwise I think it's wrong to do it without permission."
David, 14

Photos online

There's another aspect of photos that isn't usually covered by the law, and is less dangerous but still important: taking a fully clothed 'innocent' photo of someone and putting it online. Many

people find it really distressing when this happens and if you feel negative about any aspect of your appearance it can feel horrible to know that someone took a photo and shared it without your permission. I know of young people who find social times at school really unrelaxing because they are worried about people taking and sharing photos without their knowledge or permission.

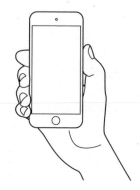

 "I saw a photo of me online recently – something my work had put up on our website. I was shocked and annoyed because I didn't like how I looked and no one had asked my permission."
Barbara

Ethics and feelings

Again, laws differ around the world, but I want to focus on ethics and feelings. You have the right to feel safe at school, during organised activities and with your friends. This means, in my opinion, that if a photo is being taken you should have the right not to be in it if you don't want to be; and if it has already been taken you have the right to say that it shouldn't be shared, particularly online. Schools usually have policies involving permission forms, which mean that you can opt out (or your parents can opt you out) of any photos being taken by an adult in the school or at school events. But this doesn't stop your peers taking photos, and that's where the problems can start.

"I would not feel comfortable with just anyone (except friends) having a picture of me on their phone but at the end of the day I don't care too much because I'm always careful with what I put out there."

Aquilat, 14

I talked to people of all ages about this and the general view was that it's usually wrong to share photos or videos without permission or knowledge unless you are quite sure that the person won't mind. It may not be against the law (unless they are sexual, involve nudity, or were taken in a private place), but it can be upsetting, stressful and nasty. If this is something that you feel isn't being dealt with properly in your school or your friendship groups, see if you can talk to someone who feels the same and then see how you might tackle it so that everyone can feel safe and relaxed.

Parents also put photos of their children online. I think this should be only done with consent, although it often isn't. I recommend you discuss with them what you're happy with. After all, would an adult like you sharing a photo of them online if they disliked the photo?

"I would be really worried if a friend takes a picture without my consent, especially if they put it on social media. This is my identity and I would like them to ask how I feel about it first."

Nana Kwame, 14

Summing up

Your body is yours and you are in charge of it. You can use it to display your personality, experiment with ways of showing off the bits you like best and minimising the effect of the bits you like least. It can be your canvas and your display board and reflect your personality and tastes. Treat it well and allow it the chance to reflect the respect you have for it. It's your brilliant body: let it shine.

RESOURCES FOR
THIS CHAPTER

ONLINE

Consent: www.girlscouts.org/en/raising-girls/happy-and-healthy/happy/what-is-consent.html

Article about consent, aimed at parents of much younger children than you but still very useful: http://adrielbooker.com/teaching-kids-body-privacy-personal-agency-consent/

ThinkUKnow re consent (UK): www.thinkuknow.co.uk/14_plus/need-advice/sex-and-the-law

For honest information about drugs, see Talk to Frank: www.talktofrank.com

BOOKS

Non-fiction

What is Consent? Why is it Important? And Other Big Questions by Yas Necati and Louise Spilsbury

FINALLY

You may have started reading this book because you dislike your body. Lots of people do, unfortunately, and probably most people don't like *something* about how they look. Or perhaps you started reading because you thought 'body image' was about how fat or thin someone is.

I hope you now see how much more fascinating and complicated the whole idea of body image is! I hope you've started to respect your body more and to value what it can do and to want to look after it so it can do even more. I hope you've discovered two main messages:

1. **Body image is all in the mind.** Your mind creates a mental picture and that mental picture is usually more negative than the reality. The mental picture produces a voice in your head and that voice is too often cruel and mean and the only person who suffers from it is the only person who hears it: you.

2. **Your body is already brilliant.** It doesn't matter what it looks like because what it looks like has *nothing* – repeat nothing – to do with your value as a potentially wonderful, successful and brilliant human being.

Finally, I hope you've learned that the best thing you can do for yourself is to *respect* yourself, body and mind. There are lots of simple ways to show that respect, whether by enjoying wonderful food, keeping your body fit and strong with exercise, or resting it with healthy sleep and essential relaxation. And the great thing is that these things are not boring chores but delicious, fun, exciting and pleasurable activities that make us feel good immediately and forever.

Your body is brilliant because of what it can do and all the things that you can make it do in the future. **Your body is brilliant** because it is the vessel for your life and your life can be great if you make the best choices and rise to meet all the challenges you meet. **Your body is brilliant** because it will do the best for you if you treat it right.

Your body is unique to you: use it well and let it be truly, positively brilliant.

Now that you've thought about this a lot, make a poster for your bedroom with your favourite inspirational quote. Here are a few from some students I worked with, but you can write whatever you want:

★ Your body is yours – own it.

★ Be confident, be creative, be classy.

★ It's your body – don't let anybody change it.

★ Pills and potions don't make you beautiful – your thoughts and actions do.

★ Happiness begins when you stop comparing yourself to others.

Index

For information about Nicola's books and events, and for lots of
advice and information, see www.nicolamorgan.com

Nicola Morgan's other books include:
Blame my Brain: the Amazing Teenage Brain Revealed
Positively Teenage: a positively brilliant guide to teenage well-being
The Teenage Guide to Friends
The Teenage Guide to Stress
The Teenage Guide to Life Online

Positively Teenage:
a positively brilliant guide
to teenage well-being

Positively Teenage shows YOU how to get the BEST out of your teenage years.

Full of practical, proven strategies for physical and mental health, *Positively Teenage* explains lots of ways to flourish physically and mentally - from doing things you enjoy to learning new skills; looking after your diet, exercise and attitude to being healthy online; getting great sleep to understanding your personality - allowing you to take control of many areas of your life.

Positively Teenage gives you the power to let yourself flourish, achieve and be who you want to be. Use your powers well! Be truly, positively, teenage! Stand tall, stretch your arms wide, take a deep breath and say, loudly (or in your head), 'I can do this!'

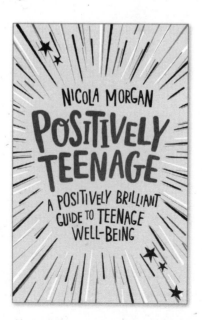